When Hope Prevails
The Personal Triumph of a Holocaust Survivor

Sam Offen

Sam Offen
"When Hope Prevails"
ggoffen@yahoo.com
248-318-4132

Artwork and Cover Design: Kimberly Franzen
Editorial Liasons: Sarah Hart and Marian Nelson

A portion of the proceeds of the sale of this book goes to benefit the Holocaust Memorial Center, Farmington Hills, Michigan.

 translated from Hebrew: remember

Library of Congress Control Number:
2005903118

When Hope Prevails: The Personal Triumph of a Holocaust Survivor /Offen, Sam
ISBN # 1-928623-58-1 (soft cover)
          1-928623-59-X (hard cover)

Summary: A personal narrative by a Holocaust survivor describing his life in Krakow, Poland before the Nazi regime; his family's experience in the Jewish Ghetto; his years in the concentration camps; and the hardships and triumphs of his life afterwards.

Printed in the United States of America.

Second Printing - December, 2009

"Choose life so that you and your offspring may live"
(Deuteronomy 30:19)

Humbly dedicated to my parents, Rochme Gitel and Jacob Offen, and my sister Miriam, as well as over fifty members of my extended family, who perished in the Holocaust. Their memories will be in my heart forever.

And to my brothers Nathan and Bernard, who shared my suffering. That all three of us survived is a rarity in the annals of the Shoah.

To my dear wife, Hyla, for her encouragement to write my life story. Little did she realize that she opened Pandora's Box. I will be eternally grateful to her for her understanding and patience.

To my daughter Gail, who so lovingly deciphered and typed my longhand writings. And my son Jerry, for his support.

Also to my children's spouses, Randy and Karen, for listening.

To the thousands of American GI's who liberated the concentration camps. Our most reliable witnesses, who proved to the world that the Holocaust did, indeed, happen.

Also to the thousands of students I have been privileged to meet, and hopefully inspire. And, most importantly, to the triumph of the human spirit.

Preface

During my time as a speaker at the Holocaust Center in Farmington Hills, Michigan, various people have urged me to write my autobiography. For a long time, I was reluctant, unwilling to face the daunting task of recreating both the worst and the best parts of my life. What finally changed my mind? In addition to serving as a survivor/speaker at the Holocaust Museum, I also lecture without remuneration at secondary schools and universities and give talks about my experiences during the Holocaust to civic groups and private companies. As a result, I have received hundreds of letters from students, teachers, and others, expressing gratitude for the opportunity to hear my story and wishing more people could have the chance to do the same. This, then, is an attempt to share the story of my life, and in that sharing to celebrate the triumph of good over evil.

Chapter 1

Childhood

I was born Salman Offen in Podgorze, a suburb of Krakow. I was born at home in my family's apartment and delivered by a midwife, wiich was the custom at the time. My mother, Rochme Gittel Offen (neé Schiffer), was twenty-four years old and my father, Jacob, was twenty-six. I would eventually be joined by three siblings, brothers Nathan and Bernard and sister Miriam. (Another brother, Moses, died twelve days after birth.)

The earliest memory of my childhood is my first day at school. My parents walked me to class, where the teacher, Ms. Czubatowa, greeted me. She was a very stout lady and apparently scared me because I started crying and refused to stay. To calm me down, my parents had to take me home. I eventually returned to first grade and the rest of the year passed uneventfully.

From later years, I remember my homeroom teacher, Mr. Przetak, who was very strict. His form of punishment was to hit anyone who misbehaved quite hard on the palms of the hands with a leather strap or belt. We boys (it was a boys-only school) invented all kinds of remedies to lessen the pain, including smearing garlic on our palms. I don't recall if this actually helped, but perhaps these efforts were of some use psychologically.

Starting in the fourth grade, study of the German language was compulsory. Since German is similar to Yiddish, I did quite well. The Christian students found it more difficult to learn a language so different from Polish, and occasionally I helped them out. My knowledge of German was to prove advantageous later on.

My favorite subjects were geography, history, Polish, and arithmetic. I attended eight years of public school, seven of which were compulsory. At that time in Poland, public education in most big cities was considered excellent, and teachers were very well respected. Teachers were so esteemed in Poland, that if you encountered one on the street, you either bowed or tipped your hat to show respect, despite the fact that they were quite strict.

In my school, three quarters of the students were Catholic and one quarter Jewish. Every morning at the conclusion of roll call, we all had to stand and listen to Catholic prayers led by the teacher. Of course, the Jewish students stood silent, but I memorized those prayers and can still recite most of them today in Polish. A couple of times a week, a priest came to teach the Catechism, and the Jewish students would go into a different classroom, where we received religious lessons from a Jewish teacher. The drawback to this inclusion of religious instruction in the school was that, of course, everyone figured out who was Catholic and who was Jewish—a situation that had consequences. Occasionally my fellow Christian classmates would beat me up or throw stones at me just for being Jewish.

For my Jewish education I attended the Talmud Torah on Rekawka Street. The Talmud Torah was an all-day school where secular subjects were taught in the morning and Jewish topics and religion in the afternoon. Because I was going to public school, I could only attend the afternoon sessions, and since those attending afternoon classes were in the minority, we were often the subjects of scorn or ridicule by some teachers and fellow students. The teachers, or *Melamed,* as they were known, did not object if afternoon students occasionally skipped classes or left early to play soccer. We were nicknamed *Goyim* or *Shagitz,* meaning "Gentile."

Most of the teachers were very strict and used a bamboo stick to discipline students. My own teacher, Reb Shaya, was more enlightened. He never beat us and yet he achieved the same or even better results, by simply paying more attention to us—realizing that we were part-time students, unlike the majority of our classmates.

*****

We were a poor but close-knit family. My mother was a house-wife and dressmaker. She was very soft-hearted and lovable, and like any other mother, she wanted her children to have a bright future. To make ends meet in a family with four children, she worked tirelessly, making custom dresses for friends and rela-tives. She often worked late into the night, and I don't remember her ever resting except perhaps on the Sabbath.

Her own early life had been one of hard knocks. She had lost her father at a fairly young age and I am sure that, as the oldest of four sisters, she had to have been concerned as to whether her wid-owed mother would be able to scrounge up enough money for four dowries, as was the custom then.

Having lived through World War I, she had suffered deprivation as a civilian, and she could not believe that when the Nazi soldiers invaded Poland they would stay very long. She, like millions of her fellow Jews, could not fathom that something like the Holocaust could possibly be in our future. How could she?

Originally a shoemaker, my father eventually became a sales-man, or peddler. Among the things he sold were cigarettes and newspapers. Tobacco was a government monopoly and a license was required to sell it. Most licenses went to army veterans. Fortunately, my father, having served in both the Polish and Austrian armies, was qualified. He also sold boxes of toothpicks to upscale restaurants, including the famous Pod Wierzynek, in Rynek Glowny (the main square), frequented by diplomats and royalty, which had even at that time been in existence for hun-dreds of years. Occasionally, he would give me a couple of these boxes to deliver, and we all helped out with sales at home (my father had created an opening in a window in our apartment which served as a sort of walk-up window).

Among the other things my father sold were school supplies and pool tables. He traveled the countryside to do this, often not even making enough money to buy a return train ticket, which meant he had to walk home to be with his beloved family for the

Sabbath. Eagerly we awaited his return. His dealing in pool tables meant that sometimes he had to store a table at our apartment until he could sell it. At those times, we were the envy of the neighborhood since we could play pool in the meantime and often invited our friends to join us.

My father could best be described as modern orthodox; he wore no beard or side locks but observed the *kashrut* laws. The Sabbath was always a festive occasion at our house, and we all attended Friday night and Saturday morning *shul* services.

Our Saturday midday meal almost invariably included the traditional *cholent,* consisting of meat, potatoes, beans, barley, or some other leftovers. Mother would put it all in an iron or clay pot and cover the top with heavy paper into which she poked small holes. One of us boys would take it to the baker on Friday, where it would be allowed to simmer for almost twenty-four hours. We would pick this delightful concoction up after *shul* on Saturday about noon and bear it home to be shared amongst our loving family. After the meal we would all sing *zmirot* (Sabbath songs), which were then followed by *bentshen* (grace after the meal). Those were joyous and never-to-be-forgotten times.

It is always with a great deal of nostalgia that I recall the holidays and festivals our family always celebrated. Passover stands out as one of my favorites. In addition to getting some new clothes, it was always a festive occasion. Father would go to the bakery with freshly laundered, large pillow cases and fill them with round matzos. Hard-boiled eggs were popular, among other foods that were unique for this particular holiday. We used to play a game not unlike marbles, but with filbert nuts, outdoors. It was the first sign of spring. Of course, the most important religious part of Passover was the Seder, which commemorates the Hebrew's exile from slavery in Egypt. The Seder was conducted by our father the first two nights, sitting on his favorite chair with a large pillow. It lasted until way past midnight, with a festive meal right in the middle. Most of my younger siblings would fall asleep.

Yom Kippur, the holiest day of the year, was quite memorable too. It was a day when we asked God for forgiveness. On the eve of Yom Kippur, either on the way to or in the synagogue, it was customary for a younger man to ask an older man for pardon, even if it was the older one who was in the wrong. It was a very nice gesture, regrettably rarely practiced nowadays. Yom Kippur commences at sundown, and ends the next day at sundown. You pray and abstain from food. Boys up to age thirteen and sick people could abstain from fasting. I had difficulty fasting at times as a teenager, having stomach aches and headaches—not unlike low blood sugar. Interestingly, since liberation, I have no problem fasting on that holy day.

We used to stay in the synagogue the whole day praying. Curiously, one of the most fervent prayers was pleading with God, hoping to be able to pray again next year. The prayer book lists about a dozen different ways in which one could meet his maker—one being by fire. Could that have been a predestination of the Holocaust?

Succoth, to commemorate the harvest, was a fun holiday because we got to show off our talents in decorating our *succah* with keen competition from neighbors and friends. Customarily, only males had their meals served there by the female members of their family. Consequently, they too competed in preparing the best meals served on the finest dishes.

Purim, though a minor holiday, was enjoyable and beneficial too. We got to dress up in costume (my favorite was Mordechai) and a face mask (not unlike Halloween) and went door to door singing Yiddish songs and receiving coins and sweets. Another custom was for families to send baskets or trays of sweets or fruit, called *shalach-manos,* to other families. Delivering it resulted in receiving more coins. Being enterprising always resulted in earning a few extra dollars or zlotys, as the Polish currency was called. And on Hanukah, inevitably we ate latkes and played the dreidel game and received only one modest present.

I have to confess that after the Sabbath meal, I would occasionally sneak out to play soccer with my brothers and friends. It was always a calculated risk, because if my father found out he would mete out just (never too severe) punishment.

It was also customary to visit relatives after the Sabbath meal. Sometimes we visited my mother's sisters and brother, who lived in our general vicinity, but the visits I remember most are those to my great-aunt Surah, who lived on Jozefa Street in the old Jewish district of Kazimierz about two miles away. She kept live chickens, which she sold at the local market, in cages in her apartment. Other times we visited my great-uncle Jacob Schiffer, who lived in the city center on Florianska Street, and was a struggling landscape painter who sold his work on street corners. (In 2004, my brother Bernard located one of his paintings in Krakow, but was not allowed to bring it out of the country since it qualified as an antique.) At least once, we traveled thirty miles to my great-uncle Leibisch Schiffer's small farm in the village of Okocim.

Both my parents were literate in Polish and Yiddish and I often saw them reading newspapers late in the evening. A veteran of both the Austrian and Polish armies, my father was considered a somewhat worldly person. Consequently, our apartment or the courtyard, depending on the weather, was frequently a hub of political debates with friends or relatives. Although these discussions seldom gave rise to any definitive solutions, it was always a great deal of fun to listen to the diverse opinions. Hence, my passion for politics.

The courtyard was also where we built our temporary *succah* hut and marked Rosh Chodesh, greeting the new moon at the beginning of every month. The apartment balconies overlooking the courtyard were at that time glassed in to keep out snow and rain. I spent many an hour playing hide-and-seek in that courtyard while the smell of noodle soup with beans wafted down from open windows. I was good at hide-and-seek. Little did I know how important that skill would turn out to be.

My maternal grandmother, Cywia Schiffer-Zwirn, who was illiterate but smart in her own way, owned a store that sold candy, ice cream, and fruit. Since it was located near my school, I occasionally worked there. During the growing season, Grandmother would get up at dawn and walk for two miles to the peasants' fruit market to purchase the freshest and best produce available and "schlep" it to her shop on Dlugosza Street. She did this for years, even at an advanced age. When her daughter Chaya was about to be married, Grandmother gave the shop as a dowry to Chaya's prospective husband, Jozef Markowicz, and retired. Being somewhat of an educated man, my uncle decided to change the way the shop was run. He installed a telephone and used it to order everything, including the ever-so-important fruit. He also hired an accountant. Within a short time he was bankrupt. It broke Grandmother's heart.

Herself a most lovable person, Grandmother adored all of her ten grandchildren and the feelings were mutual. In retrospect, I think it helps to have a Grandmother who owns a candy shop.

Besides Chaya, who had two red-headed children, my mother had two other sisters. Bayla married Meyer Gottreich of Wisnice, a small town not far from Krakow, who had come to Krakow looking for work. Grandmother, needing extra income, had turned part of her home into a boarding house. Meyer was one of her boarders, and that is how he and Bayla met. He found a job in a tannery, and they later had two children. The youngest sister, Itka, worked as a hat maker downtown. She and her husband, Leon Rosen, who was a furrier, had no children, perhaps because they were married just before the war. Itka was only a couple of years older than I.

My mother's only brother, Joel Schiffer-Zwirn, lived with my grandmother in the same apartment house that we lived in at Krakusa 9 in Podgorze. Uncle Joel, a shoemaker by trade, was an ardent Zionist and numbered among his friends such well-known Zionists as Parnes, Lieberman, and Sonnenschein, to name just a few. He had completed his *hachshara* training in preparation for eventual settlement in Palestine, but he would not leave his widowed mother or sisters. He was very well educated in Yiddish and Hebrew. He had a good voice and was assistant cantor during the high holidays in the Lorya *shul* we attended on Limanowska Street. He was much in demand for other events too, including the Purim *shpiel* (carnival) at the Talmud Torah. I recall him riding on a decorated horse in a Mordechai costume during a Purim parade.

Since Uncle Joel was single and only a few years older than I, we had a lot in common. He often played soccer with me and my brother Nathan at Krzemionki Park. On several occasions, we lost track of time and I was almost late for Cheder. Not to worry! My Uncle Joel always took out his pen and wrote a note in Yiddish to my teacher Reb Shaye at the Talmud Torah, always finding a good excuse for my tardiness. Needless to say, when my father found out, I was scolded, or worse . . .

Since Uncle Joel was the breadwinner for his family, money was a perpetual problem. Marriage brokers (*shadhan*) tried to find him a matrimonial prospect in a better financial position than he. Finally, in the mid-1930s, he became engaged to a young lady from a seemingly wealthy family named Spokojny, from Proszowice. Since I was the oldest child in the family, my parents decided to take me along to the wedding. It turned out to be quite an adventure and a lesson in life for a young teenager.

The whole family boarded a train going to Kocmyrzow, where we changed to a narrow gauge railroad to Proszowice. We were met at the station by the bride's family and transferred to several decorated, horse-drawn carriages accompanied by a klezmer band. Upon arrival at the bride's rather large house, we were greeted by more of her relatives and friends. The house was very festive with tables laden with all kinds of food, obviously prepared for a *simcha* (party). After we had a chance to rest and have some refreshments, it was time to get down to serious business. Apparently, the amount of the dowry had not been previously established. Some very hard bargaining was initiated on both sides. The go-between was my Uncle Jozef Markowicz. There were offers and counteroffers. The figures escape me, but I do remember that American dollars were mentioned. At one time, Uncle Jozef threatened to call the whole thing off, and told us to prepare for the return trip home—the marriage would not take place. I imagine it was a ploy on both sides, or perhaps part of a game to achieve maximum benefits. Finally, very late at night, an agreement was reached, and there was a big display of emotion with everyone hugging and kissing. Interestingly, throughout these proceedings, the prospective bride and groom did not even see each other. Apparently, they had no say in the matter.

The wedding was an elaborate feast with food, drink, and music. There was also a *badhan* (storyteller) present, and he made up stories and songs about almost everyone there, always in rhyme. We all had a grand time into the wee hours of the morning.

Eventually, Uncle Joel and his wife moved back to Podgorze and lived on Kalwayjska Street. They had two children. It would be nice if, like most stories, there was a happy ending and "they lived happily ever after." Unfortunately, my uncle and his family perished in the Nazi Holocaust. Now, over sixty years later, I often recall with nostalgia some of the events I shared with Uncle Joel. I loved him dearly.

My father's family originated from Dabrowa near Tarnow, about fifty miles east of Krakow. Regrettably, I never knew much about his family.

My sister Miriam, named after our paternal grandmother, was a pretty, petite girl who did well in school. As boys do, my brothers and I used to tease her, but only lovingly. She was also a very fussy eater. One of her dislikes was butter. Mother was quite upset about her eating habits. I remember one occasion when Mother, trying to add some nourishment to Miriam's school lunch, inserted a tiny bit of butter between her bread slices. It backfired because Miriam detected it, did not eat her lunch, and came home crying.

Winters were quite severe in Poland, but I enjoyed winter sports like skating and sledding down steep hills. Summer was my favorite time of year. At an early age, I used to go to a Jewish day camp located in a suburb of Krakow, called Blonie. It was quite an adventure to take the streetcar to get there; other children going to camp took the same route and we all had fun singing together. In my early teens, I went by train to a regular overnight camp for one month. It was located about fifty miles from Krakow in a resort town near Zakopane, called Rabka, which was known for its supposedly curative mineral salt water. The water was bottled under the name Solanka. The camp was located outside of town, and every morning we had to walk to the town center, metal cup in hand, and drink that awful-tasting liquid from a spigot in the town square. Otherwise, I had a great time and made new friends from different parts of the city. (In 1985, when I returned to Poland with my family, we looked for the spigot but couldn't find it. A local lady directed us to a location outside of town where the mineral water was flowing from a pipe. We all tasted it and my family confirmed my first impression—it still tasted awful.)

Another favorite vacation happened when my father earned some extra money and our family of six spent a part of the summer together. He rented a room in a farmer's house in a village outside of Krakow, near Kalwaria and we spent a whole month together. Father went back to the city on Mondays but always returned for Sabbath and would bring us candy or other goodies. We missed him and always eagerly awaited his return.

One year, during the depression, my father was employed by the Krakow municipality. Because of that connection, he was able to send me to a Boy Scout camp near the town of Ojcow. I was the only Jewish boy there. I participated in all kinds of sports and athletics that I was not familiar with, including BB rifle shooting contests. My team even won a few prizes in various events. I also learned some survival tactics, which became invaluable later on.

For some reason, Jewish homes at that time were generally devoid of pets. I managed to bring home a cuddly kitten, which I loved and enjoyed showing to my friends. It even slept with me. When Father found out, he gave me a few days to return it. Reluctantly, I obeyed. I missed that black and white ball of fuzz for a long time.

At age thirteen I had my Bar Mitzvah, signifying in our religion that I became personally responsible for my deeds. After service we had a very modest *kiddush* (meal), unlike most of the present ones which include rather elaborate parties.

Being short for my age, I was nicknamed *Myszka* (little mouse) by my classmates. Because I looked so young, I had a hard time finding employment, unlike some of my friends who had found work and were collecting wages. Yearning not to be dependent on my parents for pocket money, I did all kinds of odd jobs—I worked as a tennis boy, in an ice cream cone factory, and in my grandmother's candy shop. I also worked some evenings in the cloakroom of a well-known café named The Royal, on Gertrudy Street. Our neighbor Wicek Hilfstein patronized it and occasionally would take me there, where the owners allowed me to help out with chores, including selling cigarettes. A lot of my spare time was spent in the library since I was always an avid reader on a variety of subjects.

Several months after I left school, one of my father's friends who owned a fur shop named Fakler Furs at 15 Grodzka Street, located in the center of the city, agreed to employ me as an apprentice. The pay was nominal, but finally I had a regular job. In the mornings I worked in the shop, gaining the practical knowledge of working on furs, and in the afternoon I attended a vocational school. I spent three years learning about how to design and make a fur coat, the different tanning methods, the varieties of fur and their durability, as well as further formal education.

My real aspiration was to become a dentist, but knowing that my parents could not afford to send me to the university, I had to give up this goal. Becoming a furrier was the furthest thing from my mind. However, I had almost no choice in the matter. Becoming an apprentice in Poland, as elsewhere in Europe, meant that I had the lowest entry job and was taken advantage of in various ways. I had to walk the proprietor's children to school, and sometimes I had to bring them lunch. I had to keep the shop clean, and on some Friday mornings, it was my job to take chickens to be slaughtered in the kosher manner by a *shohet* (a ritual slaughterer). Although I detested many of these chores, as I learned more and more of the skills of the furrier trade, I began to like and enjoy it. Later in life, it afforded me a comfortable living.

The small factory where my aunt Itka worked as a hat maker was also located on Grodzka Street. One day all the workers there declared a sit-down strike and refused to leave the premises for several days. I recall bringing Itka food that Grandma had prepared.

There were myriad Jewish organizations in Krakow, including many different Zionist clubs advocating training in both self-defense and agriculture to prepare for the eventual emigration to Palestine. Although in my teens I attended quite a lot of these meetings, I did not participate actively because I did not want to part with my family. There were also Socialist organizations, like the Bund, which advocated that Jews should remain loyal Polish citizens, while opposing the right-wing government. Most of these clubs also had dances and that was the place to meet members of the opposite sex. Occasionally, individuals who were active in these Bund clubs, including some of my friends, were deemed "dangerous" by the Polish government and taken into custody.

Prior to World War I, Poland had not existed as an independent country for over 120 years. Instead it was occupied and governed by three neighboring powers; Germany (or Prussia) had control of the western part of Poland, Russia the east, and Austria the south, which included the city of Krakow and the area known as Galicia. Of all three powers, Austria was the least oppressive to Jews. However, marriages performed by rabbis were deemed illegal by the state. Since my maternal grandfather was very religious, he insisted that he and my grandmother be married by a rabbi. Consequently, my mother's birth certificate states that she is the "illegal" daughter of Shlomo Zalman Zwirn and gives her mother's surname as Schiffer. Even my mother's marriage certificate states that she is an illegal daughter. (Anti-Semitism has existed for millenia, but I'd rather not dwell on that.) When Poland gained its independence in 1918, marriages solemnized by rabbis were again recognized as valid.

Zalman Zwirn came from a long line of rabbis. An orphan, he rebelled against this heritage and became a shoemaker. After being discharged from the Austrian army, my father got a job as an apprentice in my grandfather's shop and that is how he met my mother.

I never knew my grandfather, who died before I was born, but in my teens I was told by some of his peers that he was a very learned man, humble and well respected. Incidentally, the name Zwirn means "sewing thread" in Yiddish. My father's family name, Offen, means "open."

There is an interesting story about the Offens. I have blue eyes and don't look typically Jewish. The explanation for this may lie in the seventeenth century, when marauding Swedish soldiers occupied the Krakow area. Chances are that one of my forebears may have been one of those soldiers. (In fact, to this day, the name Offen is listed in the Swedish telephone book.)

World War I concluded in 1918, and in 1919, Poland regained her independence through the Treaty of Versailles. Prior to 1795, Poland had been an empire that included parts of Lithuania, Belorussia, and the Ukraine. In the early part of the 1920s, Poland, under the command of its hero, Marshal Josef Pilsudski, decided to re-conquer some of these territories. For this, troops were needed, and my father was conscripted into the Polish army. Pilsudski's quest was victorious as parts of the lost empire were re-annexed to Poland, a situation that lasted until the German invasion of 1939. My father possessed a silver cigarette case that bore an inscription signed by either Pilsudski or some other general that cited his bravery in battle. He was very proud of it and would have been sad to learn that we later bartered it for food in the Krakow ghetto.

Perhaps because he was really a soldier and not a skilled politician, throughout his tenure different factions secretly tried to overthrow Pilsudski's government. But, because he had control of the army, he ruled until his death, becoming a sort of benevolent dictator. Still, during this period, citizens enjoyed some freedom, although that did not extend to the publishing of anti-government articles. The government censors must have worked overtime, because quite frequently the police would come to the window where we sold newspapers and confiscate them, no questions asked or answered.

Some Jews also prospered during Pilsudski's regime, and we prayed for his well-being. We constituted about 10 percent of the population (of thirty-five million) and made many important contributions to Polish life in the fields of medicine, law, literature, commerce, etc. Szymon Ashkenzy, a Jew, represented Poland in the League of Nations from 1920 to 1923. I do not recall many Jews being active in the national government, but I do remember Dr. Ozajasz Thon being an outspoken and well-respected member of the Polish SEJM, or parliament, in Warsaw, representing Krakow. Once or twice I went to listen to his most outstanding speeches.

Marshal Pilsudski died in May 1935. I still remember his funeral in Krakow. People stood in line for hours watching dignitaries from all over the world walk behind the silver casket with a glass top and sides containing his embalmed body, his famously large, drooping mustache still visible. His coffin was taken to Wawel Castle, which dominates this royal city and former capital. Most Polish kings and queens were crowned and entombed there. I, like millions of others, went to view his enshrined body. It is still on display.

After Pilsudski's death, different factions struggled to gain control of the Polish government. General Rydz-Smigly's strong nationalist and anti-Semitic party came to power. Anti-Jewish demonstrations ensued, urging Poles to boycott Jewish shops. At the universities, quotas for Jews were instituted. Those who attended had to sit in the back of the class, or the "bench ghetto" as it was nicknamed. Occasionally there were riots in which a few Jews were killed.

We learned to live with it. We had no choice. Besides, there was little we could do to withstand the semi-official, government-supported propaganda.

As the summer of 1939 began, ominous war clouds loomed over Europe. Hitler threatened Poland with invasion. Anti-Semitism was rampant in Germany. Earlier that summer, my father's uncle unexpectedly knocked on our door. Born in Poland, at an early age he emigrated to Germany. He married and settled in Berlin with his German-born children. One day, the Gestapo came to his door and ordered the whole family to pack their suitcases, leave everything else behind, and report to the train station. The train took them, along with hundreds of other hapless Jews, to the east. Their journey terminated right on the Polish border, where they were brutally ordered to exit and found themselves in the "no man's land" between Poland and Germany. There were no facilities of any kind, and they had only the food they had managed to bring along in their suitcases. They lived in those conditions for a few days because the Polish government at first refused them entry.

Eventually, some Jewish organizations were permitted to help them and that is how they found themselves in Krakow. My great-uncle and his family gave us a first-hand account of what was going on in Nazi Germany and the hair-raising conditions Jews had to endure. It was quite an eye opener. For the first time, fear and trepidation entered our lives. If this could happen in Germany, could it happen in Poland?

Our fears were intensified as Hitler threatened to invade Poland if the country refused to relinquish a corridor across Poland, giving Germany access to the "neutral" Baltic port city of Danzig. Poland refused. The government assured its citizens that they had nothing to fear and claimed that the Polish army was mightier than Germany's. In fact, Poland was about to sign a treaty with France and England, guaranteeing that they would come to Poland's defense if Germany invaded. The Polish government even went so far as to ask its citizens to put radios in their windows so passersby could hear about the treaty after it was signed in late August. During the last days of August, we heard planes flying overhead and some anti-aircraft artillery going off in the distance.

The Polish authorities claimed these were just maneuvers. One morning, Nathan found what looked like a piece of metal and showed it to our father. Father confirmed that it was indeed a piece of shrapnel. He knew that armies seldom, if ever, practice with live ammunition, and feared that war was imminent.

Being in his mid-forties, Father was too old to be drafted into the Polish army. I had just turned eighteen and was too young to serve. Some of our eligible friends and relatives were called up for service and came to say farewell wearing their army uniforms.

One of them was Mother's cousin by marriage, Ignac Traubman, a tinsmith by trade. The streets were teeming with soldiers in uniform. The bulk of the Polish forces were heading west to the German frontier. Most were marching or riding horses, although there were some tanks and motor vehicles. Unfortunately, my father had been right.

Chapter 2

German Invasion

Friday, September 1, 1939—a very ominous day. The Nazi armies invaded Poland. That evening, my mother lit the Sabbath candles with tears in her eyes. She prayed more fervently than ever that we be spared the ravages of war.

My father, fearing that the Germans might induct him into the German army because he had served in the Austrian army, packed a suitcase, and together with other Jewish males, joined the remnants of the Polish army, which was retreating east toward the Soviet border. He had second thoughts the very same day and returned home, saying he could not abandon us, and that together we would share our future, come what may. The Polish army fought bravely but ultimately could not withstand the Germans. The retreating soldiers opened up some warehouses and the populace helped themselves to some of the merchandise. We obtained a few boxes of chocolates. Fearing the German soldiers' intoxication habits, the Poles emptied most of the alcohol from the barrels into the Vistula River.

In the aftermath of the invasion, both newspapers and radio essentially ceased to exist. We had no official information whatsoever but learned from never-ending streams of retreating soldiers arriving in Krakow from the front that the situation was hopeless. With the government ineffective, our apartment house, like many others, organized a neighborhood watch to keep peace among our fellow dwellers.

How well I remember that small group of neighbors. The families who lived on the first floor included the Goldsztofs, who had three children, the middle of whom was my friend Baruch, who, like my father, was sent east and was never heard from again; Mr. Lerhaft, who owned the apartment building and was somehow related to a cousin of mine; the Katz and Hofsteter families, each of whom had five members; and Mrs. Kenerowa and her son Wicek. The ground floor was occupied by an umbrella shop run by Mr. Wachtel, a Czech citizen who was taken away by the secret police just days before the outbreak of the war; Mr. Blonski's butcher shop; and the Goldsztofs' grocery store. There, too, lived an old maid, Miss Spingarn, and Tzanger the beggar. We lived on the ground floor, and the Bernhut family lived on the second floor. Mr. Bernhut owned a *doroszka* (horse carriage) and often took us on rides on his way to the stable. The Bernhuts had a daughter, Salwina, and four sons. I remember three of the boys, Józek, Salek, and Moniek. (In the late 1980s I met Józek in Los Angeles. He and I, along with my two brothers, are the only inhabitants of that apartment building who survived the Holocaust as far as we know.)

The Nazi army entered Krakow on Wednesday, September 6, and from that day on, life changed completely. There was total chaos in the city, stores and factories were looted, and there was a general fear of the brutal Nazi SS. Immediately, the Nazis instituted a strict curfew, according to which Jewish people were not allowed to leave their homes. After a few days, as food supplies ran out (in those days we had neither refrigerators nor freezers stocked with food), hunger started to set in. After several days, the Nazis relented and lifted the curfew for daytime only, allowing us to go out and buy food. Everyone had to stand in line for hours just to obtain a loaf of bread. Since there were four of us, we would all stand in line and chances were good that two or sometimes even three of us got a loaf and thus were able to share it with our older relatives or friends who could not stand in line. We were forbidden to use public transport. Later on we were prohibited from walking to the city center or parks lest we contaminate the non-Jewish inhabitants because we were deemed "diseased."

But lifting the curfew proved to be a cruel hoax by the Nazis.

Once we were able to walk the streets of the city and mingle among them, they immediately began harassing, beating, and killing us for one reason: we were Jews! One of the first brutal Nazi crimes I witnessed involved the orthodox Jews known as Chassidim. The Chassidim wore distinctive black coats and hats and were also recognizable by their beards and side locks. One day, while I was out searching for food, a group of young Nazi SS soldiers rounded up a group of these hapless Jews and put them against a wall. One soldier pulled a pair of scissors out of his pocket and attempted to cut the side locks off one of them. When the poor fellow got scared and tried to run away, another soldier pulled out his gun and killed him right on the spot.

Over the coming years, I would witness many more horrors, but even today I am still unable to fathom how anyone can kill a fellow human in cold blood. When I was young we were told that World War I had been the war that would end all wars. It was now clear that this was naïve. The Nazis quickly instituted an inhumane regime. Everybody—men, women, and children—was put to hard menial tasks like shoveling snow, unloading freight cars, and cleaning out homes and apartments that had been confiscated from Jews to make room for the ever-swelling arrivals of more high ranking Nazi officers.

In particular, the Nazis were searching for young, able-bodied males for forced labor. My father, fearing for our safety, decided to take Nathan and me to his cousin's farm. (It is a misconception that Jews were not allowed to own land in Poland. There were many Jewish farmers and landowners.) This cousin, Hillel Green, owned a very large farm in the village of Czarkowka, which was near Staszow, perhaps fifty miles north of Krakow.

We left Krakow on a small steamer that plied the Vistula River. We disembarked in Staszow, and then walked a few miles to the farm. Happily, we did not encounter any German soldiers. Even though we arrived unannounced (there had been no way to contact them in advance), the Greens agreed to house us until it was safe to return to Krakow. Father left us there and went back home to be with the rest of our family.

The Green family consisted of two sons and a daughter, who were just a little older than we were. They welcomed us warmly and were very generous. They all worked on the farm with the help of most of the villagers. Hillel, with his long gray beard, looked very majestic behind a horse-drawn plow.

They knew about the Nazi atrocities we had endured in Krakow and for our sake hoped that this situation would soon pass. The Germans had not yet invaded their area, food was in abundance, and life went on pretty much as usual. Once a week a *shohet* would arrive and prepare enough meat for the week, and every Saturday we would walk to a different farmhouse in the area for Sabbath services, which were followed by a sumptuous *kiddush*.

We lived on the farm for a few weeks, ever anxious to know the fate of the rest of our family, but there was no way to communicate with them. One day, with great sorrow, the Greens informed us that a traitorous peasant had tipped off some Germans in the area that the Greens were harboring Jews from the city (it seems that the Nazis, realizing they needed food for their troops, had decided for the time being to leave Jewish farmers alone). For our own safety, and perhaps theirs too, we had to return to Krakow. They packed us some food, all that we could carry, and with tears in our eyes we said goodbye. We set out for Krakow to share in our family's fate. We never saw the Greens again. Somehow we were lucky enough to elude the German patrols marauding in both the countryside and the city and managed to find our way home. Our parents and siblings were elated to see us alive, and vice versa.

The food we brought with us was most welcome since constant shortages had become a fact of life. We also got chilling news about the loss of some of our relatives and close friends. Killings and deportations were happening almost daily. The SS would bring big trucks to our neighborhood and, with no questions asked, fill the vehicles with Jews and drive away with their human cargo. We never saw those people again. And we lived like this for about one and a half years. In addition, all Jewish-owned shops and businesses were confiscated without any compensation and given to the "new owners"—Nazi party members. Schools ceased to exist for the Jews. The ultimate objective of the Nazis was to allow Polish children to be educated up to the fourth grade so that they could be servants for the master race. The Polish intelligencia was thus decimated.

Chapter 3
Krakow Ghetto

In March of 1941, all the Jewish people remaining in Krakow were ordered to move to a ghetto that was established in our suburb of Podgorze, on the south side of the Vistula River. Originally there were rumors that the ghetto would be established in the Kazimierz district—an old Jewish historical area which contained many ancient synagogues and Jewish-owned shops. People were allowed only about two weeks to move. All you could bring with you were the possessions you could carry on your back or in a cart. Inevitably, panic ensued. Some went into hiding. Others tried to obtain papers identifying them as Aryan. It was an unbearable experience. Society then was much less mobile and some families had lived in the same dwelling for several generations. (By this time, Jews had been living in Poland for hundreds of years.) It was heart-wrenching to suddenly be confronted with an order to vacate a beloved home with so much history attached to it, knowing you might never return.

My family did not have to move because our apartment was within the ghetto walls. Luckily, our family of six was still together, but now we had to take in two or three other families, as the Nazi order forced some thirty to forty thousand oppressed souls into an area that measured about one square mile. At times, we had ten or fifteen people quartered in our two-room apartment. But this did not turn out to be our worst problem. Under Nazi oppression, hunger and disease ran rampant. According to the standards of the International Red Cross, we were supposed to receive a minimum food ration. I found out later that we actually received less than half of that requirement. Never during my internment in the ghetto or in the concentration camps did the International Committee of the Red Cross bother to check on our hopeless conditions. Was this blatant omission an anti-Semitic occurrence? Unfortunately, to this day, the International Red Cross does not recognize the Red Magen David Adam, the Israeli Red Cross, although it does recognize the Muslim Red Crescent. Furthermore, almost every day the SS or other soldiers came into the ghetto and committed all kinds of atrocities, including murder. Once we were all settled in the ghetto, new problems arose. In order to be allowed to reside in the ghetto and to receive the meager food rations, you had to have an identification card, called a *Kennkarte*. To qualify for this document, you had to be employed by a German concern but, of course, the Nazi authorities discouraged anyone from employing Jews. This catch-22 situation was serious, because if you did not get an identification card, you faced expulsion or deportation from the ghetto. If you could not obtain a card legally, you could sometimes buy one—many of the Germans were not averse to bribery.

The best jobs were those the Nazis required for the war effort. Needless to say, the occupation of furrier was not considered essential, so on my application I stated instead that I was a mechanic's helper. Although this was no guarantee of a job, I did find work, sometimes as a laborer unloading coal or cement from railroad cars, other times cleaning out apartments that the Germans had confiscated or working at the army barracks. Mother, Father, and Miriam all worked at the Madritsch clothing factory, a large building next to our apartment building (it was a former chocolate factory named *Optima*), making uniforms and boots for the German army. Nathan got a job at a brick factory in Bonarka, a suburb of Krakow (Jews were allowed to leave the ghetto to work provided they were under guard). Bernard had to hide—he was too young to obtain one. Fortunately the five of us obtained *Kennkarten* legally.

Despite so much suffering, the Jewish people rarely lost their sense of humor. Gallows humor was common, and several lighthearted songs were composed about our plight. Here is one I remember (unfortunately, when translated into English it doesn't rhyme like the original):

> Even though the Jews say veto
> There will be a Ghetto.
> Everybody will be here
> And should someone object
> No *Kennkarte* will he get
> Who can stop him living this way?
> There will be a Jewish district
> With a Jewish post office and police
> And there will be a Jewish jail
> For anyone who steals,
> There will be a Jewish laborer
> And a Jewish doctor
> There will be a Jewish pharmacist
> And a Jewish porter.
> Oh, and we will have *tzures* (problems) here!
> Such *tzures* and *Kennkarten!*
> This is how it is going to be
> The simple truth
> That's the Ghetto
> The Krakow Ghetto here!

One day, a group of Storm Troopers broke into our apartment, creating chaos by yelling and screaming in their customary fashion, ordering all of us to leave. My father, detecting that the group's commanding officer had an Austrian accent, told him with tears in his eyes that he had served in the Austrian army with distinction in World War I and begged him to spare us. Without a word, the officer ordered the other soldiers out, and thus we avoided certain execution. This was one of the extremely rare occasions where a Nazi showed a trace of humanity.

Food smuggling was rampant in the ghetto, but since currency was worthless, gold, jewelry, clothes, and other household items were used as barter and there was a thriving black market. Few of us had much of value. Jewelry or furs were one of the first items seized by the Nazis under the threat of death. While several of us tried our hand at smuggling, it was Bernard who was most active in this endeavor. Because he was only twelve, he could fit in through the smallest holes in the barbed wire surrounding the ghetto. He would sneak out once a week—sometimes more depending on how tightly the ghetto was guarded. It sounds like an adventure, but in reality, it was a very risky endeavor. Bernard soon learned to spot the blue-uniformed Polish policemen who guarded the gates. They were often bribable, which made his task less dangerous. We all had to wear the Star of David on our right arms and anyone caught outside the ghetto walls without permission was easily identified. The consequence of that was certain death.

As our resources dwindled, earning money or finding something to barter for food became a top priority. Sometimes we heard of jobs that rewarded workers with food instead of the worthless "ghetto marks" with which Jews were paid. Our most prized possession was a silk needlepoint picture of Moses as a child in a reed basket being rescued from the Nile by Pharoah's daughter. Set in an exquisite gold frame, and measuring about three by five feet, it had been embroidered by my mother and hung in a prominent place in our apartment. In desperation, we found we would have to part with this treasure. Luckily, the man we found to help us was Wladislaw Cieslik. A Polish Christian, born in America, he managed the Helvetia chocolate factory in Krakow, and aided many Jews during this horrible time, often at great risk to himself. In my family's case, he gave us food in exchange for the needlepoint picture and said he would keep it safe. When we gave it up, my mother had tears in her eyes and we all made a solemn promise that if any of us survived the war, we would attempt to retrieve it. I still hope someday to find it.

Cieslik's actions are a reminder of the humanitarian sacrifices some Polish people made, at the risk of losing their own lives, by hiding Jewish people in their homes or on their farms. We even bartered for food with them outside the ghetto, which was forbidden. Indeed, thousands of Poles were honored, some posthumously, by Yad Vashem, the Israeli Holocaust Memorial, for their noble efforts.

Regrettably, there were also those who betrayed Jews, either for material gain or because of anti-Semitism. The reward for betraying a Jew was equivalent to five kilos of sugar, a carton of cigarettes, or something else of approximately the same value.

In June of 1941, Germany, despite having earlier signed a non-aggression pact, invaded the Soviet Union. Even in our dire situation we experienced a moment of jubilation, hoping that the tide of war would reverse—that the Russians would finally stop the Germans. After only a few days, we realized how premature our rejoicing was. The Germans started gobbling up hundreds of miles of Soviet territory. This victory seemed to embolden the Nazis, who really put the squeeze on us and our lives became even more dangerous. Our already meager food rations were cut and much more forced labor was demanded.

By this time, the Germans had started to send their damaged trucks and other equipment for restoration to various conquered places, including Krakow. I was "fortunate" to get a job in an old Polish factory located in a suburb called Rakowice. I worked alongside a Polish mechanic as a helper, and occasionally he would give me a loaf of bread or some other foodstuff that I was able to take home to my hungry family.

Whenever we went to work outside the ghetto gates, the Nazi guards walked alongside. Occasionally someone managed to escape. If the Nazis found out that anyone had gotten away, upon our return to the ghetto, they would shoot one of us for every one who escaped—a macabre tit-for-tat.

Once they invaded the Soviet Union, their manpower diminished, and they instituted a devious new plan of self-policing that required fewer guards. We were made to walk out of the ghetto in lines of five or six and told to watch one another in order to prevent the escape of any individual person. If one escaped, the whole line would be shot. Imagine our feeling, having to police ourselves and watch a brother or a friend as a means of self-preservation. Apparently, that cruel system worked because I do not recall any escapes once this procedure began.

By now the ghetto had been halved in size because of the constant loss of its inhabitants to starvation, disease, deportation, and Nazi killings. By some miracle, my family was still together, living in an apartment reduced to one room. Most of our possessions had either been bartered for food or confiscated.

Winter of 1941, cars with loudspeakers entered the ghetto and announced that all Jews had to turn in their furs and fur-trimmed coats at the Judenrat (a sort of city council on Limanowska street appointed, ironically, by the Gestapo and consisting of prominent Jews who were still alive). Noncompliance was punishable by death, as was the breaking of other inhumane regulations. As all winters in Poland were severe, we were cold and shivering when forced to go to work.

Then came October 28, 1942, a date I will never forget. As we walked out of the ghetto to our jobs, I saw an unusual number of Nazi soldiers with machine guns, dogs, and trucks. I sensed that something terrible was going to happen.

On that ominous morning, my brother Bernard had slipped out of the ghetto to barter for food and my father had left the apartment (at this time he and Bernard usually worked at home repairing shoes). Nathan was working nights at a railroad siding in the suburb of Zablocie.

While at the station the night before, Nathan had had an encounter with the Nazis. The Germans were bringing their wounded and frozen soldiers back from the Russian front by train, and Nathan was one of several Jews at the station who were ordered to carry the soldiers across the railroad tracks to an *entlausing* (delousing) car, where they were to receive medical attention. One young German SS called to Nathan in broken Polish, calling him "friend" and asking him for help. Thinking that the man was no "friend" of his, Nathan nevertheless picked him up and carried him on his back to the railroad car. The SS man screamed in pain, and Nathan thought, "Good, serves him right," a thought he immediately regretted, thinking that to wish the Nazis pain was to sink to their level.

In the morning, Nathan and the other Jewish workers returned under guard to the ghetto. As they reached the bridge over the river, they could see a large number of trucks heading into the ghetto. At Plac Zgody (now called Heroes' Square), more trucks and SS were assembled and there, to his dismay, Nathan saw our mother, with Miriam holding her skirt, terrified. Nathan tried to reach them, but the man guarding them struck him with his rifle butt, smashing both sides of his face. Mother motioned for Nathan to run, but the guard grabbed him and dragged him away.

At the same time that my mother and sister were rounded up for deportation, patients and staff at the Central Hospital on Jozefinska Street were murdered. The Nazis went in and started shooting on the spot anybody they encountered. Nathan saw some SS troops pick up little babies by their feet and throw them out the window; others smashed the babies' heads against the sidewalk outside. My brother and others had to pick up the corpses and load them onto trucks and horse-drawn wagons and then walk alongside as the bodies were taken to a site outside the ghetto, where hundreds of people, some of them still moaning, were thrown into mass graves.

When the last transport arrived, the SS started shooting at Nathan and the other commandos, probably hoping to wipe out all witnesses to their crime. Seeing what was happening, my brother jumped into the grave. Covered in blood, he pretended to be dead. He stayed there all night and when things had calmed down, he crawled out from under a heap of bodies. Fortunately, he found somebody willing to help and give him some new clothes, and so he struggled home.

Bernard in the meantime had returned from his bartering mission, but could not get back into the ghetto because it was so heavily guarded.

Having spent an anxious day at work, I returned and encountered a most horrible sight. The streets were literally strewn with bodies. The Nazis had massacred hundreds of women, men, and children that day. I ran to my apartment but no one was there. I was frantic to discover what had happened to everyone. Eventually, Bernard and my father returned, but it soon became clear that my mother and sister had been among those picked up for deportation.

After liberation we found out that they had been sent to either the Majdanek or the Belzec extermination camp. They did not survive the gas chambers. My sister was only fourteen, my mother forty-five.

My father was never the same again. Such was our situation that we were not even allowed to mourn the greatest tragedy in our lives.

The Nazis, under the command of Governor Hans Frank, decided to make Krakow the capital of German-occupied Poland. Their plan was to make the city *judenfrei* (free of Jews) for the first time in several centuries. Those of us remaining in the ghetto were ordered to build a so-called labor camp in Plaszow on the site of a Jewish cemetery—another instance of cruel irony in the Nazis' twisted scheme!

Chapter 4

Plaszow Concentration Camp

Building the barracks for the camp was back-breaking labor, made worse because the Nazis wanted it done speedily. Before we could begin, we had to desecrate the graves and knock down the monuments. There were bones and skeletons all around us. It was a gruesome scene, but on the threat of death, we could do nothing to protest. Finally, when the camp was ready, we were ordered to walk to Plaszow, under guard, in March 1943. Plaszow is the camp portrayed in the movie *Schindler's List,* and anyone who has seen the film will recall the constant killings that took place on that infamous march. Once we settled in Plaszow, it became clear that the "labor camp" was in fact a concentration camp with electrified barbed wire surrounding the perimeter, machine gun towers, and search lights. *Schindler's List* captures some of the terror and hopelessness of our situation, but in reality, it was much worse. Perhaps the producers were skeptical that the public would believe that any of this actually took place. I empathize with their predicament, for I, who was there and lived to tell the disbelieving world about it later, still cannot believe that this actually happened.

The commandant of the camp was Amon Goeth. Goeth was the most bestial Nazi I came across during my entire ordeal. He personally killed countless people with his revolver and with his ever-present telescopic rifle as shown in *Schindler's List*, while his underlings killed many more using more "efficient" methods.

Every morning at dawn, rain or shine, we had to assemble on the camp square and wait, sometimes for hours, until a Nazi official would come to count our noses. They wanted to know exactly how many people they had killed the previous day or how many had died in the barracks of hunger or disease. In one corner of the square they erected a gallows, and they constantly hung people, especially teenagers, for all kinds of invented "crimes." Commandant Goeth personally administered the *coup de gras* by shooting the victim in the head after the hanging.

I remember in particular one of many ghastly hangings, that of Mr. Krautwirth, a prominent Krakow engineer. His so-called crime totally escapes me. For some reason, the rope broke, and Mr. Krautwirth fell to the ground. He begged Commander Goeth to spare him, pleading his innocence, but unfortunately to no avail. He was picked up by the guards and hung all over again. All of the assembled had to watch these savage proceedings—we weren't allowed to avert our eyes. The guards walked between our lines, making sure we kept our heads up. We were terrified!

The gallows were never taken down, but loomed over the camp with a rope dangling in the open air as a very frightening reminder to all of us of what could happen to anyone at any moment. No one ever knew who might be the next victim and the randomness of this horror only increased our sense of terror.

Most of the executions in Plaszow were carried out in a place nicknamed Hujowa Gorka, literally meaning "Prick Hill," nick-named after a vicious killer—an SS officer named Huyar. Summary executions there were the norm. It was an old Austrian fortification, used by the Polish Army between the two World Wars, surrounded by a deep ravine. It contained thousands of bodies, including some Jewish Kapos from the ghetto and their traitor-ous chief, Simcha Szpira. (The Kapos' main function consisted of supplying the Nazis with slave laborers. They also made lists of people to deport—which meant certain death.) Also executed on this spot were the Jewish police chief of Plaszow, Wilek Chilowicz, his wife and family, his deputy, M. Finkelstein, and his other brutal assistants. This was the payback for their cooperation with the duplicitous Nazis. In 1943-44, the Nazis ordered us to exhume all those bodies, pour gasoline over them, and burn them to ashes. They did not want to leave any traces of their brutality. The stench and smoke were unbearable.

Since the camp had become a prison, those of us who had been there a while wore striped uniforms that had numbers stamped on them instead of names. It was another way to dehumanize us. Goeth came up to the camp from his villa (where he often held drunken parties) accompanied by two vicious dogs. He would sic the dogs on the first prisoner he encountered. Those dogs were trained to jump at you, bite, and eventually pull you down to the ground, where Commander Goeth would again administer the *coup de gras* and kill you. One day I was working alone, fixing the road with a shovel. Suddenly, out of the corner of my eye, I saw the commandant and his dogs approaching me and realized that these might be the last moments of my life. Everyone who hears this story wonders why I did not try to run away. There was no place to go: the concentration camp had hundreds of armed guards. Occasionally, a prisoner would try to escape because he or she was at wits' end and could not endure the brutality of camp life any longer. But even if that prisoner were lucky enough to elude the guards, he or she would still be electrocuted on the barbed wire or killed by a tower guard.

As was his custom, Goeth sicced the dogs on me. I still don't know what was in my mind at that particular moment, but as the dogs jumped and snarled, I continued to work with my shovel, trying not to pay attention to the attack, which seemed to last an eternity. Luckily, the dogs were unable to pull me down. Something about my resistance must have appealed to Goeth. He ordered the dogs to let go, and walked away. Thus I became the first prisoner to survive the attack of these vicious dogs. After Goeth left, I was bleeding profusely. There was an infirmary of sorts at the camp, but to go there was tantamount to death, because the guards would periodically inspect these premises and machine gun everyone they encountered there. I managed to get back to my barracks, where, at great personal risk, a Jewish clinic attendant, who had heard through the grapevine of the attack, applied iodine to my wounds and bound them in bandages. I still have dog-bite marks on my hip and left thumb, a reminder of my first near-death encounter. Little did I know then that many more would follow.

In their quest to conquer the Soviets, the Germans took hundreds of thousands of prisoners of war. Some of these prisoners volunteered to help the German cause and became guards at concentration camps. The Soviet Union consisted of many ethnic groups, and the prisoners who served as guards at our camp were Ukrainian. They were even more brutal than the Nazis, if that was possible. They tried to out-master their German counterparts in their vicious deeds. They spoke little German and their orders or commands were hard to understand. Perhaps thinking they had been disobeyed, many became trigger-happy and decided to shoot first and ask questions later.

Another level of authority we had to deal with were the Kapos, both in the ghetto and in Plaszow. Kapos were Jewish volunteers, with a knowledge of the German language and very low moral character, who agreed to help the Nazis. They were instrumental in supplying the Nazi tormentors with Jewish labor from the ghetto and helping to select people for transport to the death camps. Mistakenly, they thought that by performing these dastardly deeds they would save themselves. However, when a new commanding officer took charge and wanted his own underlings, Kapos were often executed.

In Plaszow, among other duties, the Kapos were in charge of the distribution of our meager food rations. One could not afford to offend them, because their dislike was equivalent to death. There was no appeal to a higher authority.

One Kapo at Plaszow was a third-generation German-born Jew. He bemoaned the fact that he had never known that one of his grandparents was Jewish. Under Nazi law, you were considered Jewish if one of your grandparents was Jewish. Despite his position, he was a decent human being. Perhaps because we could converse in German, he would sometimes give me, clandestinely, an ever-so-important extra slice of bread. Yet, he was a typical German and followed orders to a tee. I do not know his fate. Regrettably, I missed him when he was transferred to an unknown destination.

Plaszow functioned as a sort of headquarters for the Nazis' use of Jewish labor. From there, we were sent to different subcamps, factories, salt mines, wherever the Nazis needed slave labor, for several weeks at a time, eventually returning to Plaszow.

Ever-present at Plaszow was a young SS guard called Willi, who was a vicious killer. One day, my best friend Mietek Pfeffer (his parents had owned a small shop in our apartment building) and I were stringing up barbed wire for a small holding camp inside the main camp. Along came Willi, and we started trembling. Willi said to me that Mietek was working slower than I was and that he deserved punishment. Since Willi was the sole judge and jury, he decided that I had to administer fifty lashes on Mietek's bare bottom. He gave me his lead-tipped whip and ordered me to administer the blows, but they had to be hard ones, or else they would not count. With a heavy heart I proceeded to carry out the order. But how can you be so inhuman and whip your friend? Some of my lashes were not to Willi's liking, so he did not count those, and I had to do it all over again. When I finally finished that gruesome task, Willi turned to Mietek and asked him ironically why I was so cruel and whipped him so hard. He told Mietek to take revenge and whip me just as hard, which Mietek reluctantly did. Normally, after such an encounter, Willi took out his revolver and killed both men. Luckily for us, he just walked away. Some time later, I found myself in that very same camp behind the barbed wires. It was used as a holding camp for those about to be transferred to another camp, or so we were told. My uncle, Leon Rosen, was in the holding camp with me. I had some kind of an insect bite on my forehead, and he suggested that I go to the officer in charge and show him, perhaps thinking it would be wiser for me to stay in Plaszow, rather than be deported to an unknown location. Uncle Leon practically pushed me toward the Nazi officer, who yelled, "What's wrong?" I showed him my forehead and he immediately ordered me to leave. I would later learn that everyone in the holding pen had been taken to a different camp and executed, including Uncle Leon. Once more I had eluded certain death.

During my time in Plaszow, I had several assignments, including working on road repairs, wheeling the bodies of executed prisoners to the burial pit, and pulling wagons overloaded with rocks. There were several light industrial concerns in the camp which were run by German civilians but controlled by Nazis. One of these made white fur coats for the German army to use on the Soviet front so they would blend in with the snowy terrain. By a stroke of good luck, the Jewish manager of that establishment was no other than my former employer, the furrier Maciek Fakler. He would frequently request that I be employed there, rather than doing the jobs I mentioned above. Working in a warm barracks during the harsh winter months helped my precarious existence. One day, a high-ranking Nazi officer came into the fur barracks holding a cage containing two live foxes. He ordered us to make a fox collar for his girlfriend and told us that, if the job was satisfactory, he would let us keep the meat as a reward. We had not eaten meat of any kind in months. First, we had to dispatch the foxes, but by that time we were so hardened that killing an animal seemed simple. Apparently, the officer was content with the finished product, and we feasted on fox stew. I don't remember the taste, but surely it must have been the best meal I had in a long time, and probably it prolonged my life. The idea of fox stew seems repugnant to me now, but out of necessity, humans can and do adapt to life's circumstances.

Interned with us at Plaszow were a father and two teenage sons who were very religious. On Yom Kippur in 1943, the father met a tragic end. For Jews, Yom Kippur is the holiest day of the year and one on which we abstain from food for twenty-four hours. The father was quite ill, and on Yom Kippur he was found dead in the latrine, clutching a slice of bread. Had he been willing to desecrate this holy day and eat the bread he might have cheated death for a few more days. Many other Jews in the camp risked death to pray and maintain the Jewish rituals.

No one can speak of Plaszow without mentioning Oscar Schindler, who single-handedly saved over a thousand Jews from

Goeth's blood-soaked hands by using them as laborers in his business. Schindler bribed Goeth by, among other things, supplying him with alcohol. Although I wasn't one of the individuals Schindler saved, a fair number of my friends and schoolmates were among them.

Plaszow was the second largest concentration camp, after Auschwitz, in the Krakow area. Jewish Kapos in uniform were forced to hang Polish political prisoners brought to Plaszow from the Gestapo prison on Montelupich street. They filmed the gruesome scenes and used them for propaganda to incite the Poles against the Jews. Our sadistic Ukrainian guards took advantage of our dire situation too. Their century-old hatred of Jews caused untold pogroms.

Our barracks were built with thin boards. The same wooden boards were nailed together in one continuous line three tiers high to serve as our beds with no mattresses. There was no heat or water. Much later, latrines were built, with cold water only.

At the onset there was no organized labor in Plaszow. Since there was a quarry in the camp, the Nazis once again invented a cruel way to keep us busy. We had to pick up large rocks and run with them to deposit them a few hundred feet away, on a neat pile. The next day we had to return the very same rocks to their original place.

In the ghetto a number of Jewish doctors were killed because they refused to supply the Nazis with the names of sick people. In Plaszow the same situation occurred. Dr. Gross, a Jew, was in charge of the camp hospital. Frequently the Nazis demanded from him a list of very sick people likely to die soon. They wanted to execute them in order not to have to feed them any more. If Dr. Gross would not obey, he and all the patients would face execution. Fearing for his own safety and that of his charges, he supplied them only with the very oldest and sickest—those likely to expire soon. After liberation, some survivors blamed him for the loss of their loved ones and accused him of cooperating with the Nazis. He was put on trial in Krakow, found guilty, and hanged. Afterwards, other survivors claimed that by using his method, Dr.

were already in eastern Poland and should be approaching Krakow in the near future. That gave us great hope that the years of suffering under the Nazis might finally come to an end. We were not celebrating yet, since we were still at their mercy, but this news gave Nathan and me and two or three friends enough hope to develop an escape plan. We hid some of the extra food the Poles gave us in unused caves and decided that if it seemed liberation was imminent and the guards came down to the mine to evacuate us, the five of us would hide in that cave. One day, the guards quite unexpectedly came down to the mine and ordered an immediate evacuation. Nathan and I were unable to follow through with our plan and were taken to the top of the shaft with the other Jewish miners. From there, we were immediately taken back to Plaszow.

We later found out that our collaborators—Fuchs, whose father had owned a tannery and who lived in our apartment house in Krakow, and Spielman, whose parents owned a bakery and who had lived around the corner—had managed to hide in the cave. Unfortunately, the Nazis went down to the mine with search dogs, found them, and took them back to Plaszow, where they were hanged. By sheer luck, Nathan and I, though not by our own choice, were spared our dear friends' tragic fate.

Chapter 6

Mauthausen and Gusen

Once again, the Germans outwitted us. On a very hot day in August 1944 (as depicted in *Schindler's List*), we were forced to enter cattle cars in Plaszow. They kept pushing us in until there was standing room only, shoulder to shoulder. We had no food, water, or toilet facilities (you had to perform all your natural functions on the same spot), and people were dying all around us. By coincidence, Father, Nathan, Bernard, and I found ourselves in the same cattle car but, unfortunately, as fate would have it, not for very long. I remember "celebrating" one of my birthdays in that cattle car on August 7, 1944.

We journeyed for a few days and when we reached our destination many of our fellow travelers were dead. Fortunately, the four of us survived this horrendous journey. Upon disembarking, we found out that we were in Mauthausen, Austria, another concentration camp. Even then, we had no respite. Many people had died on route and the survivors were forced to carry the bodies from the cars to the camp—a gruesome task. Emotionally, I was totally drained and also I was physically exhausted, not having had any food or liquid for some three or four days. Confusion, depression, fear, and anger accompanied us. Was this our last journey just because we were mere Jews? This uncertainty was our constant companion. The brutal Nazis were masters in instilling fear in our daily "lives."

After a process of disinfection and registration, miraculously we were still together and had a brief moment to reflect on our future and, of course, mourn the loss of our loved ones. We all looked bedraggled and emaciated, but we could hardly recognize our father. He was only forty-nine years old, but he looked seventy.

Tragically, we were soon forcibly separated. Bernard, who was fifteen, and our father were sent away, destination unknown. We did not have a chance to hug or kiss or even say goodbye, and I had an uneasy premonition that I would never see them again. Nathan and I remained behind, quartered in a temporary camp and expecting to be transferred somewhere else. We were given striped uniforms, some with bloodstains, no underwear or socks of any kind, and old, dilapidated, ill-fitting shoes. We waited in fearful anticipation of what would happen next.

We were soon assigned to slave labor at the infamous stone quarry in Gusen. Our job consisted of running down 186 very steep steps, picking up a big stone, running up to the top of the quarry, and depositing it there. All day long, run down, run up with a big stone on our shoulders. The guards did not even have to waste bullets to kill us. All they had to do was push us from the top of the quarry to our deaths. Despite the hard labor, our rations were extremely meager, so much so that we were in fact starving. In the morning we received a bowl of warm black "coffee," at noon a bowl of thin soup, and at night a slice of bread, period. That was our total diet. I remember a group of totally emaciated inmates sitting on the barracks floor, discussing what each wanted to become if we were ever liberated. Needless to say, there were different ambitions. But when my turn came, I expressed a desire to work in a restaurant for the rest of my life, so as never to run out of food. We were so hungry that we took great risks to get the smallest morsels. I noticed that when taking their lunch break, the SS guards would smoke cigarettes and eat apples, throwing the cores on the ground. I occasionally tried to retrieve those cores. Fortunately, I was never apprehended for committing that "crime."

Also interned in the camp at Gusen were some Austrian Quakers who had refused to carry arms for the Fatherland. By some lucky coincidence, I was picked to occasionally clean their barracks. This gesture undoubtedly saved my life and perhaps that of others, too. Other than losing their freedom, the Quakers had an almost normal life. They were prisoners but had all the food they needed. In addition to receiving food packages from their families, they also received mail. This was in the spring of 1945, but we had no idea that the war was almost over. We still heard planes flying overhead, followed by anti-aircraft artillery. When an alarm sounded we were chased to an air raid shelter dug deep in the mountains. It also served as an enormous warehouse and aircraft factory to avoid being destroyed by the Allied bombers. The Quakers informed us that the Allies were advancing rapidly, and that if we could hold out a while longer, we would be saved—this information was a great psychological lift. They also gave me some extra food, which I shared with Nathan and some fellow inmates. By now we were nothing but walking skeletons and this bit of food helped us to survive.

In both Mauthausen and Gusen we had to deal with a different kind of Kapo. Now we faced Kapos who were hardened criminals. They were German citizens who instead of going to prison had been sent to concentration camps to become our tormentors, a task in which they excelled. The Kapos were in charge of our daily sustenance, and they were not averse to drowning inmates in a barrel of water in order to increase their own rations. They didn't report these deaths to the Nazi authorities, who didn't care anyway.

Another deadly feature we had to face was the weekly shower. The winter of 1944–45 was very severe. We had to walk under guard totally naked with no shoes in deep snow to the shower barracks some distance away. Most of the time the water was cold, no doubt deliberately, and to compound our misery we had no soap or towels and we had to return to a cold barracks, our skin frozen. The lack of soap, combined with the filthy condition of our living quarters, led to us also being covered with lice. We were constantly scratching our skin and we developed painful sores on our bodies. Since so many inmates were already in fragile physical condition, the shock of these cold showers weakened them even further. Many succumbed to disease and died.

Acute diarrhea, vomiting, and dehydration sapped the little strength we had left. We "lived" with death constantly and were constantly humiliated. In the mornings on the way to the latrine we found many corpses lying on the ground. The skeleton-like bodies could not even make it all the way there. We, the "living" ones, were ordered to pick them up and stack them like wood.

Although the Nazis must have known that their reign of terror was coming to an end, they nevertheless tried to kill as many of us as possible in the final days. They were so bloodthirsty that nothing could stop them. In early September 1944, a group of us consisting of about three hundred prisoners was sent to Gusen. At the time of liberation, about eight months later, only about five or six of this original group were still alive, including my brother Nathan and me. The rest all perished. And, of course, because the Nazis sent in replacements almost daily, the actual death toll was even higher. Had my liberation come a few days later, I would not have survived!

Chapter 7

Liberation

In early May, we were marched from Gusen back to Mauthausen. Something was up, but we didn't know what. On the morning of May 5, 1945, there was an ominous silence outside our barracks. There were no shootings, guards screaming, or dogs barking. We were not quite sure what was happening, but we were too scared to investigate. Later, we learned that all the Nazi guards had escaped the night before, just ahead of the advancing Allied armies. A short time later, about a half dozen American tanks and halftracks stumbled upon our camp. The soldiers were bewildered at the sight of so many unburied corpses lying on the ground and shocked to see what looked like living skeletons weakly welcoming them. They had no idea that they had just liberated a concentration camp and knew nothing about German atrocities. Very few of us spoke English, but some of the soldiers spoke Polish or Yiddish, and we were able to inform them of our plight. They, in turn, told us that the war was not yet over, and they had to continue to pursue the enemy, but they left us with plenty of food, cigarettes, chocolate, anything edible.

Liberated at last! After all those long years of living in hell and the constant fear that at any moment one might be killed—the relief and joy was indescribable. For the first time in years, people saw food that they had only been able to dream of. Some made the mistake of gorging themselves, but because their bodies could not absorb the rich foods that the generous GIs left us, they suffered from diarrhea and related disorders. Some even died. What a pitiful way to go after so many years of inhumane suffering, unable to control your own destiny at this crucial juncture. Despite our hunger, Nathan and I ate very little of that rich food. We were afraid of the consequences.

Our camp consisted of inmates of many nations, but many were basically political prisoners and were not treated quite as harshly as Jews were. We were simply slated for annihilation. When the American GIs left the camp with a promise to return and bring help, my hopes were shattered. Were the tanks a mirage? My confusion increased. I was hoping that it was not a dream, and that the real nightmare was over, and that the Germans would not return, thanks to my liberators.

Finally, several days later, help arrived. I could not emotionally believe that we were free at last. I knew the conditions in the camp, but freedom was confusing. What would happen next? It really took some time for me to believe that our suffering was finally over. For the first time in perhaps two years I saw my face in a mirror. Another fear entered my mind, since I did not recognize my face; could a skeleton like me ever return to a normal life?

It has been almost sixty years since that happened. I cannot exactly recall the feelings that I had. But the exhilaration that went on, the shouts and cries . . . . It is absolutely indescribable. I wish I could recall it more vividly than I do right now. But, time has elapsed . . . . I just can't be as jubilant as I was at that time. On May 5, 1945, I told my children, it was like I was reborn!

The stronger inmates started celebrating our newfound freedom. Nathan was very weak from an almost fatal beating he had received earlier from a brutal Kapo, and we were barely able to partake in the euphoria that followed. My thoughts were elsewhere. Free at last and lucky to be alive, but what price did we pay for our freedom? Where was the rest of our family? Did any survive? Were Nathan and I the only ones left? The unthinkable questions gnawed at our minds. But one must never give up hope. However elusive, hope was the only choice we had left.

The first couple of days after liberation were chaotic, and we had to fend for ourselves. I, being the stronger one, went scrounging for food at the neighboring Austrian farms. Most would not even open the door for me, but others gave me some scraps, thus enabling us to stave off hunger until organized help arrived. Finally, after almost six years of living hell under the merciless Nazis, I looked forward to the future.

Within days, the American army returned with bulldozers and dug big trenches on the camp grounds. The officers rounded up as many officials as they could from surrounding villages and towns. They brought them to the camp and showed them the hundreds of unburied bodies lying around. The officials disclaimed any knowledge of what transpired in the camp. Of course they were lying, because the SS guards were their brothers, spouses, or other relatives. How could they not know? We were led through their towns guarded by the SS and beaten with their rifle butts in front of the locals. It came out later how happy these people had been that this camp was built near their town because the location was a high unemployment area and was quite remote. Finally, the Americans ordered them to pick up the bodies, one by one, and place them gently in the mass grave. There was visible disgust and hatred on their faces. To avoid contamination and disease we were sprayed with a white powder to be deloused. Later we found out it was DDT.

Much later I learned that the original purpose of this camp had been to house mentally or physically handicapped children. In pursuit of their twisted ideal of a pure and perfect "Aryan" society, the Nazis took such children away from their parents and sent them to Mauthausen and other institutions like it. Some of these "undesirable" children died (or were killed) and their bodies were sent to the crematorium built at Mauthausen in the 1930s. The ashes were returned to the parents, who were told that their child had died of natural causes. In the early years of the war, the camp was expanded, the first inmates being Soviet POWs. Some downed American pilots were also interned there.

Shortly after this forced burial, the American army erected a big field hospital where both Nathan and I started the healing process. UNWRA, a United Nations-like organization, started registering survivors and making the lists available. We pored over thousands of names on those lists but regretfully found none of our relatives. But we were still hopeful, because it was early in the post-war era. Physically we were getting better and were able to walk, but barely. After a few weeks at the US hospital, we were moved to a displaced persons camp in Linz.

Chapter 8

Post-War Travails

Now we had to decide what to do. Should we (could we) return to Krakow? What were our options? My first reaction was to return to Krakow, hoping miraculously to find my family who may not have registered on the survivors list but physically were not yet able to travel. There was also the abhorrent thought of my family being so brutally and methodically murdered by the Nazis not so long ago. My mind was just beginning to realize the enormity of this tragedy. I was unable to make a decision. I wasn't even sure if our apartment was still standing and if it was, I knew that it most likely no longer belonged to us. In the meantime, a trickle of survivors who had gone back started to return with horror stories. Their return was most difficult because of lack of proper documentation plus the fact that they had to cross a few borders before reaching the displaced persons camps in Austria or Germany. Since there was no regular communication, we found out through friends that they did not encounter any of our family.

The thought of returning to Poland was abandoned, at least for the foreseeable future. Palestine became our next goal. Since I had some training in future emigration there, called *hahashara*, it seemed like a splendid opportunity. The training took place on the fields Blonie. We used broomsticks in place of guns for self defense and learned rudimentary methods of farming on hot, dry, parched land. Little did I realize then the circuitous route I would be forced to take, due to unexpected and tragic circumstances, to reach Palestine, the future state of Israel. I still remember the slo-

gan used by some Polish anti-Semites: "Jews go to Palestine."
Some survivors wanted to go to Palestine, and we considered it.

Chapter 9

Attempting to Reach Palestine

In 1945, Palestine was occupied by the British under a League of Nations mandate. Since the British had close ties with the oil-producing Arab nations, they did not want to offend Arabs, and were allowing only a trickle of Jewish immigrants to reach Palestine. To help the Allied cause, they had reluctantly allowed Jewish soldiers from Palestine to form a brigade that became part of the British Eighth Army. They distinguished themselves and fought bravely all over Europe.

Clandestinely, the Jewish Brigade formed a sub-group known as Bricha, whose main object was to smuggle the surviving remnants of the European Jewish population into Palestine. Nathan and I were approached and, after some deliberation, decided to try to start a new life in what we hoped would be a future independent Israel.

Survivors who wished to go to Palestine gathered in port cities throughout Europe, while Bricha struggled to find ships for the journey. Most of the vessels they managed to obtain were not even seaworthy, but the desire of the would-be immigrants was unflinching. The British warships set up a blockade, but some of the vessels managed to reach shore. Those traveling on ships that did not make it were forcibly taken to camps in Cyprus. Eventually, they were released, and bowing to international pressure, eventually permitted to go to Palestine. These groups were instrumental in later forming the state of Israel.

Although free at last after almost six years being so close to death at any moment, I must admit that on our trip to Italy (en route to Palestine) I was very apprehensive to enter either a truck or train because they were the vehicles that led ultimately to a death camps. For a long time I was afraid of showers too, because of the fear of the gas chamber. Being greeted with such warmth by the Italian people on the train platforms, instead of brutal SS men with their vicious dogs yelling and screaming, gave me my first real sense of freedom. Ultimately we were taken to the fishing port of Ancona on the Adriatic Sea. Living on a beach in tents in Ancona, almost destitute, I began to appreciate freedom at its best. Yet, encountering a man in a uniform caused a sense of panic. (Perhaps by later joining the Polish Army I initiated a healing process of all my fears.)

Since we lived on an isolated beach and did not speak Italian, there was not too much communication with the locals, who caused us no concerns. Much to our relief, all the years of very hard slave labor mercifully ceased. Some boredom set in, but we compensated the idle days by exercising, swimming, and listening to some older more knowledgeable survivors lecturing about Palestine, and hoping to eventually join them there. On some nights we had a small camp fire and danced and sung Hebrew, Yiddish, and Polish songs. We were waiting for our dream ships. There were perhaps twenty or thirty of us. It was a very memorable time. We had no close friends or relatives there. We wore hand-me-down clothes. Food was scarce, and we lived mostly on canned food brought irregularly by truck. Sometimes we received a few packages of British cigarettes. On occasional forays to a local village, we were able to barter cigarettes for fresh fruit or vegetables, which helped in varying our dull diet. To warm or cook our food, we made fires on the beach, which we were cautioned to keep small so as not to bring attention to our presence. We had no salt, so we used sea water instead. The truck driver never talked to us, except to tell us to keep waiting. But we understood the reasons for secrecy. We were waiting for a starless night when a ship could sail into port unseen and take us to our longed-for destination—Palestine. It was now a couple of months after liberation, and we found ourselves still living in utter poverty and growing tired of waiting.

Chapter 10

Joining the Polish Army in Exile

One day, Nathan and I ventured into town. There we encountered two soldiers in British uniforms speaking Polish. They were just as surprised as we were by this encounter. After some conversation, they invited us to accompany them to their base which was located outside of a town named Jolanta. Once there, they introduced us to the officer on duty, who invited us to his tent. It turned out to be a Polish Army field hospital. To satisfy our curiosity of how they came to be there, he told us the history of the Polish Army in exile.

Before the war began, the Jews of Poland constituted the largest minority group within the total population, and consequently there were a fair number of Jews in the Polish armed forces. When Poland fell in September of 1939, the Soviets immediately annexed Eastern Poland, as per a previous secret pact with Germany. When the Polish forces were routed by the Germans, the remnants of the army, unaware of that traitorous pact, withdrew to the east, where they were captured and taken to Soviet POW camps (some of these POWs were executed in the infamous massacre at Katyn, originally blamed on the Germans, but now known to be a Soviet action).

In 1942, with the Germans at the very gates of Moscow and St. Petersburg, the Soviets reluctantly agreed to Allied suggestions that they free the Polish POWs, who were, after all, experienced fighters. The US and Great Britain even agreed to equip them. Like Pharaoh and the Hebrew slaves of Moses' time, Stalin decided the best course of action was to let the Poles go. They were transported by train and truck via Persia (present-day Iran), Iraq, and Syria to Palestine, where they became part of the British Eighth Army under the command of General Wladyslaw Anders. (Once in Palestine some Jewish-Polish soldiers deserted. The most famous of the deserters was none other then Menachem Begin, the future prime minister of Israel.)

As part of the Eighth Army, the Poles were instrumental in the invasion of Sicily and the drive up the Italian peninsula. Among other venues, they distinguished themselves in the fight for the monastery at Monte Casino, where, although they sustained tremendous numbers of casualties, they were able to reach the summit, thus opening the road for the Allies to reach Rome and other parts of Italy.

The officer who told us this story was himself a Jewish doctor, and he told us that other doctors serving in the hospital were too. We were the first survivors he had met. He had only a limited grasp of the enormity of the Holocaust, but knew it was a great tragedy. We spent a few hours in his tent comparing notes about our families. We also met some of his fellow officers. All of them were concerned about our future, which did not look bright, and they came to the conclusion that since the fighting was over, it might be a good idea for us to join the Polish Army in exile for the foreseeable future. After lengthy consideration and with the help of the Jewish officer, we joined the army. We figured that we could always go to Palestine later on.

To the best of our knowledge, no other survivors joined the Polish Army. Food was plentiful. We received regular army pay and were assigned to light duty. We even guarded German POWs held temporarily in a cave surrounded by barbed wire, ironically very much reminiscent of some of the camps we had been imprisoned in. They were allowed to come out of the cave to smoke, which they did profusely. I was armed with a British Tommy gun and kept my finger on the trigger, lest they try to escape. As we eyed one another warily, I was dying to let them know that I was Jewish and that our roles had finally changed, but we were forbidden to communicate. After a few days, I began to fear that I might be overcome with emotion, and that there might be an "accidental mishap." I asked for and was relieved from further guard duties.

The army officers were still concerned about our health and we were sent to a sanatorium to further recuperate. Since the sanatorium was in Barletta, on the Adriatic Sea, we were taken almost daily to the beach by Jeep. The doctors continued to monitor our progress and ultimately they declared us fit. After a while, we volunteered for basic training. I guess that my knowledge of Polish language and history were deemed sufficient, because I was offered a commission to an army officers' school. I politely declined, claiming I was still looking for the remnants of my family. Life finally took on a semblance of normalcy.

Chapter 11

Miraculous Reunion with Brother Bernard

One summer day in 1945, as Nathan and I were walking the streets of Bari, a city in southern Italy, on the way to an Allied Jewish Soldiers' club, somebody tapped us on the back of the shoulders and cried out, "Hello Brothers!" We turned around and right in front of us was our brother Bernard.

I was shocked! I still recall that my heart was beating so fast and I was speechless for some time. When he called us by our names we knew with certainty that it was indeed our sixteen-year-old brother Bernard, whom we last saw in Mauthausen concentration camp and were so brutally separated from about fifteen months before. We looked at each other with disbelieving and tearful eyes, and started hugging in front of other soldiers. (I don't recall soldiers in uniform hugging in those days.) It was as if he had come back from the dead. We had never given up hope that we would find our family members, and finally our optimism and hope were well rewarded.

The reunion and reminiscences went on for many hours.

Bernard told us that he had heard that Nathan and I had both survived, and had started searching for our whereabouts. (For some reason he had failed to register, so his name had not appeared on any of the lists we had been scouring for survivors.)

Given the chaos that was the post-war situation, it still amazes me that Bernard was able to find us. Before joining the army, Nathan and I had traveled through Austria and Italy in a variety of conveyances so as not to arouse the ire of the authorities, always on the lookout for "illegal" persons. Bernard, who was only sixteen, had an easier time moving around since his youth tended to allay suspicions. After comparing notes, we were amazed to find that at one time he had been merely days away from our location. As it was, it took him almost three months to find us.

Regretably, the flip side to our joyful meeting was finding out that our father was no longer living. He and Bernard had both been sent from Mauthausen to Auschwitz in a cattle-car journey just as horrible as the one from Plaszow to Mauthausen.

In Auschwitz a "selection" took place, although at first they didn't realize what exactly was happening. Father was ordered to march to the left and Bernard to the right. The prisoners sent to the left were told that they were going to take a shower and had to undress before entering the building. They were told to leave their clothes in a neat pile, so they could "retrieve them later." The left line went not to the showers, but directly to the gas chamber. As those in the left line walked into the "shower" room, they were pushed along by SS men called Sonderkommandos. After about fifteen or twenty minutes, they all suffocated. Crews of prisoners were used to pull out the dead bodies and take them to the crematorium. Those crews had a short life span because the Nazis, not wanting to leave any eyewitnesses behind, would regularly slaughter them too. And thus, only eight months short of liberation, our beloved father suffered an untimely demise. It was an irreplaceable and painful loss. But Bernard, on the other hand, miraculously survived Auschwitz as one of its youngest inmates.

Thus our reunion turned out to be bittersweet as we faced the reality that although we were three lucky survivors, it seemed most likely that we had lost over fifty members of our immediate and extended families. It was finally sinking in that never again would we see the happy faces of our parents, sister, grandmother, uncles, and aunts, not to mention the giggling faces of our countless young cousins, mere children when they were murdered by the Nazis. Even the consolation of being able to visit their graves was denied us—there were no cemeteries and no gravestones, just ashes wheeled callously away from the crematoria and dumped into rivers and fields.

It was even more amazing to realize that we, as three surviving siblings, were truly a rarity in the annals of the Holocaust. It is a tragic fact that hundreds of thousands of Jewish families were literally annihilated. Not one member remains on the face of the earth, not one survivor is left to tell of his or her existence. Most poignantly, in some families no one remains to say Kaddish, the Jewish prayer for the dead.

Another problem soon arose. We did not wish to separate, and Bernard was too young to join the army. Once again, we were lucky. With some help from our comrades, we were able to quarter him with some civilian dependents of the army, not too far from our post.

In the fall of 1945, another unexpected reunion took place. On Rosh Hashanah (the Jewish New Year), we were on our way to the Allied Jewish club in Bari, when Nathan recognized another Polish Army soldier as our cousin Ignac Traubman. He had been one of the POWs the Soviets released to fight in General Anders's army. His wife and family had perished in the Holocaust. The four of us had a great celebration together with some American and British soldiers. (Ignac went to London like us, where he remarried. We would get together quite often right up until his death.)

By now we knew that careers in the Polish Army were out of the question. We were in touch with friends in the port of Santa Maria de Bagni in southern Italy, who were waiting for a ship to take them to Palestine, so that still seemed to be an option. Little did we know that our lives were once again about to change forever.

Chapter 12

Finding Unknown Relatives in America

I had long known that my grandmother had occasionally asked my uncle Joel to write a letter to someone in America. I used to run errands for her back in Krakow, and she would sometimes send me to the post office to mail those letters. Like any teenager, I was curious about the address on the envelope: Detroit, Michigan. But I never asked any questions.

One day, while discussing our future plans, Nathan remembered the name on the letters our grandmother had sent to America. It was Hirschman. In the hope that she might have been writing to relatives, we composed a letter giving our three names and some other family names and mailed it, simply addressed to Hirschman, Detroit, Michigan.

A few weeks later, the much anticipated reply came back. It was a letter in English from a Rose and Harry Saltzman. We found someone to translate it and learned that they were asking for more details concerning our family in Krakow. This letter sounded optimistic. After complying with their request and another long wait the letter we awaited so anxiously arrived. It confirmed that we were indeed related. The three of us were elated. Miraculously, we had found relatives in America. This was even more surprising when we considered that just a short time ago we hadn't an inkling of their existence, even in our wildest dreams. We were also happy to find out that it was a rather large family.

So who were the Saltzmans? And how did they end up with our letter? My grandfather, Zalman Zwirn, after whom I was named (although my birth certificate reads Salman, my Hebrew name is

Shlomo Zalman), had a sister named Anna who married a man named Hirschman. In the early 1900s, Anna and her husband emigrated to America. Eventually, they settled in Detroit and had five daughters and three sons. My grandmother was their sister-in-law, and they corresponded. The Hirschman girls married men named Saltzman, Fishman, Weinstein, Gaba, and Maisano. Our original letter from Italy found its way to the Saltzmans, who were childless. (I don't know how but in Detroit, as elsewhere, there were organizations specializing in finding and reuniting survivors. By the time we arrived in America, these organizations were already disbanded.)

Chapter 13

Life in London, England

Meanwhile, the Allied forces were departing from the countries they had occupied and returning home. We had no home to go back to. Since the Polish Army was under British command, we decided to go to England to be discharged (or "demobbed" as the Brits say). As an army dependent, Bernard was sent on ahead to London. We traveled later with the rest of the troops. This was in November 1946, and at first we weren't too happy. We did not speak English and the change in climate from sunny Italy to damp and foggy England in the autumn season was a shock. But we were hoping it might eventually become a stepping stone for our new goal—America.

After crossing the English Channel, we journeyed from Dover to the northern English town of Carlisle, close to the Scottish border. From there, we were taken by truck to a British military base. The first English they taught us was the song "My Bonnie Lies Over the Ocean." As we marched through Carlisle in our military uniforms singing that song, the populace applauded us. Of course, we did not understand the lyrics, but we felt proud anyway.

Our assignments at the base consisted of various jobs, including guard duty. Occasionally, we obtained a pass to visit the town. On one such sojourn, Nathan and I stopped at the window of a fur shop. Hesitant at first, we mustered our courage and, armed with an English-Polish dictionary, entered the shop. The proprietor greeted us, noticed the Polish insignia on our uniforms, and much to our surprise, greeted us in perfect Polish. He invited us to join him for tea in the rear of the shop, where we met his wife.

In the conversation that ensued, we learned that he was not only Polish but also Jewish. What a relief! His name was Mr. Kirschner which, ironically, means 'furrier' in German. He had an unusual background. He had left the city of Lvov just before the start of the war. He landed in London and found an ad in the weekly *Jewish Chronicle* for a furrier in Carlisle. He went there, got the job, and eventually married the owner's daughter. Kindly, he offered to let me work in his shop whenever I could spare the time. I was able to make arrangements for Nathan to do guard duties in my name so I could work there. Because I earned extra money, we were able to make occasional trips to London to visit Bernard. He was able to obtain residence in London with an extremely nice Jewish family named Lyons. They had a beautiful house in the Kensington district. They even sent him to school to learn English. He was blessed to finally be able to start a normal life after living through a horrific childhood.

We were still living on the army base. The only way to obtain discharge from the army was to get a job and housing. Since our base was located on the Scottish-English border, it took all night by train to get to London, where most of the jobs were. That difficulty was compounded by the fact that neither Nathan or I knew much English. We were lucky and eventually obtained employment. Nathan found work in a garment factory, and I got a job with another furrier.

Securing housing was difficult mainly because London was recovering from the Blitz. Once again, we were fortunate. In Carlisle, there was a social club for soldiers, the NAAFI (Navy, Army, Air Force Institutes), which is equivalent to the USO. We attended some functions there and on one occasion met an English soldier named Bert Davis, whose aunt lived in London. He spoke some German, and we explained to him our need for housing. He said he might have a solution, and several days later told us that his aunt, Miriam Friedman, a widow, had agreed to provide us with lodgings.

With proof of housing, we got our discharge papers and left for London. Mrs. Friedman lived alone in an older house containing four bedrooms. We became great friends with her family, and they practically adopted us. To our relief, she also spoke some Polish and Yiddish, so we could communicate. Once we acquired more language skills, we made some English friends and life started slowly returning to normal.

Even though Nathan and I were attending night school to learn English, we could still find ourselves in embarrassing situations. I had gotten used to smoking a brand of cigarettes called Players, which I purchased from the local tobacconist. Knowing very few English phrases, I came in one day and asked for the usual, "Twenty Players, please." The tobacconist answered, "No Players today, sorry." I hesitated and answered, "Twenty Sorrys, please," thinking that "sorry" was a brand of cigarettes. Later on, I befriended the tobacconist's sons, who explained the misunderstanding I had with their father, and we all had a good laugh. Although they were Jewish, they did not speak Yiddish. A few years later, the whole family emigrated to Australia.

A few months after this, when I had learned to read some English, I was scanning a newspaper called the *Hackney Gazette,* which specialized in want ads, and found a fur shop looking for someone with my qualifications. After a brief tryout, they offered me a position with double the wages I was earning.

In London I subscribed to a Polish newspaper and finally was able to learn about the post-war situation in Europe, and Poland in particular. In 1945–46, the Soviet Union annexed the eastern part of Poland. In exchange, Stalin awarded Poland a swath of German territory. This hundred-mile-wide area on the western border of Poland included Silesia, Pomerania, and Stettin. About six million Germans were evicted from this area to make room for millions of Poles, who were in turn being "repatriated" from what had been eastern Poland, which Pilsudski with my father and other soldiers helped conquer. Large cities that had belonged to Poland until 1939, such as Wilno and Lvov, reverted to Lithuania and Ukraine, respectively. Consequently, Poland's borders moved westward.

Most of General Anders's, Polish army in exile, including civilian dependents, consisted of over half a million people living in the west, mainly in Great Britain. Most of them did not want to return to Poland, which was run by a Communist government, fearing repercussions for fighting for the west.

In the spring of 1947, we received a letter from the Saltzmans, indicating they would be coming to London soon and were anxious to meet us. We awaited their visit with great anticipation, mainly because we were apprehensive of the language barrier, but we also looked forward to finally meeting these long-lost relatives. Luckily, they also spoke Yiddish. Our first meeting took place at their hotel. They were the most wonderful and considerate people. Inevitably, our conversation turned to questions about our perished family. They were very curious to learn as much as possible about our family life in Poland. Also, they were very interested in our plans. We told them that if possible, our desire was to get to America. They were very happy to hear that, because much to our surprise they showed us three one-way airplane tickets from London to Detroit. They were hoping that we would be able to return together to Detroit. The joy we felt at that moment defies description.

At that time in England, food and other necessities were rationed in an attempt to avoid shortages. The Saltzmans had learned of that situation and, to our astonishment, pulled out of their luggage a five-pound kosher salami, rye bread (not forgetting the mustard), and other goodies—delicacies we had not seen or tasted in years. I will never forget that feast in their hotel room.

They also had letters of introduction to a Mr. Barnett Janner, a Jewish MP later knighted by the queen, as well as to some other government officials, with pleas to help us obtain visas to travel to the US. After several days, they were informed that since we were born in Poland, we would have to register at the American Embassy in London and wait our turn, which might take up to five years. The Saltzmans were greatly disappointed, as were we. They flew back to Detroit and our correspondence continued.

As time went by, our English language skills continued to improve, as did our lives. Bernard had left the Lyons family and joined us at Mrs. Friedman's. We had come to love Mrs.

Friedman, whom we called Mitch. We joined an English-Jewish social club, which was attached to the local synagogue. We participated in various activities—dances, soccer, and even cricket. We were busy during the weekends. We would go on outings to the countryside, or "rambles" as the British call them. Life was wonderful and fortune seemed to finally smile at me. After living through what seemed like an eternity in hell, I was still only twenty-five years "young."

As my English became progressively better, it became much easier to make friends both at work and at the social club. Once a month, we attended a play in the West End, which was London's equivalent of Broadway. One of the most memorable plays was *Death of a Salesman* with the late Paul Muni. Our social club also put on plays. I once played Sherlock Holmes and had to smoke a pipe for the role. I soon gave up my cigarettes for pipe-smoking, a habit I pursued for the next thirty or so years. Saturday afternoons were set aside to attend soccer games. My favorite team was the "Tottenham Hotspurs" in the premier league.

Our local synagogue had been damaged during the German Blitz, but the British government repaired it after the war and by the time we arrived in London it was functioning once more. It was called the Rouel Road Synagogue of Bermondsey. Since the rabbi there also doubled as the cantor, I joined his choir for the High Holidays. It was joyous and very meaningful. Eventually, I enrolled in evening classes at the Royal College of Fashion and Design.

Finally, in early 1951, a letter arrived from the US Embassy informing us that our visas would be ready promptly, and to start preparing to leave for America in a certain period of time. Nathan and Bernard were elated. I was lukewarm at the idea of leaving London after almost five years full of exciting activities. I was also reluctant to leave my job managing a fur establishment, which commanded a good salary. Worst of all, the idea of parting with Mrs. Friedman and her family, who treated us as their own, was depressing. I continued to procrastinate as our visas drew close to their expiration date. My life in London was too exciting to leave.

My brothers, however, were very eager to go. They pointed out that if we didn't like life in America, we could always return to England. Some friends who had visited America said life there was very "rush-rush" and we might find it hard to adjust after the leisurely pace of London. Not wanting to be separated from my beloved brothers, I gave in and the three of us left London. In retrospect, I realized that I also knew I could not disappoint my only flesh-and-blood relatives, who were waiting for our arrival in America.

We had only ten days left before we had to be on American soil, but fortunately American-flagged ships are considered American soil and a passenger-carrying freighter meeting that description was then docked in London and had room for three passengers. Sad, but also hopeful, we sailed for America and a new life. For the first time in my life, I left a country on my own volition, without being forced or prodded to leave.

The ship we sailed on was the SS *American Producer*, a Liberty ship owned by the United States line. It carried only twelve passengers, most of whom were American or Canadian. Passengers were quartered with the ship's officers, so we dined in their mess hall on linen tablecloths served by waiters wearing white gloves. It was the most luxurious experience any of us had ever enjoyed.

Chapter 14

America the Beautiful

After a rather rough crossing, we arrived in New York harbor on a Saturday evening, the first day of spring, in March 1951. Our ship anchored near the Statue of Liberty—an impressive and wonderful sight. Our hearts were beating fast with excitement as we finally reached our elusive goal, AMERICA. The next morning, an immigration official boarded the ship, bringing us the Sunday edition of the *New York Times*. I could not believe the size of that newspaper. We spent some time with the officer, who was very kind, as he checked the validity of our visas, asking many pertinent questions, and briefing us on the procedures we would need to follow when the ship reached its final destination at the terminal.

To our great delight, Rose and Harry Saltzman were waiting at the end of the dock. The Saltzmans usually spent one month every winter in Florida. Because of our pending arrival, they had altered their itinerary and driven from Florida to New York to meet us, with the intention of then continuing on to Detroit. The reunion was an extremely happy occasion. For the first time we were able to warmly embrace one another on American soil. What a difference from our traumatic separation in London almost five years earlier.

We checked in at the (now defunct) Statler Hotel on Seventh Avenue, where we stayed for two nights. The Saltzmans spent two days showing us the sights of New York. While we were still living in London, I had learned as much as I could about America by listening every Friday night to Alistair Cooke's radio show "A Letter from America." Cooke was then an English newsman living in America, and we were fascinated by his tales, which he related in the wonderful voice that would later become well-known when he hosted *Masterpiece Theater* on public television. Still, we found New York amazing—I had a lot to learn about America.

Once we had checked out of the hotel and headed for Detroit, our conversation was almost non-stop. I wanted to know everything about our newfound relatives. Our great-aunt Anna Hirschman, who had emigrated to America and started the American branch of the family, had passed away in 1944, so, unfortunately, we did not have an opportunity to meet her. Her oldest daughter, Gertie, and Gertie's four sisters (including Rose Saltzman) and two remaining brothers were my mother's first cousins, making them our second cousins, and their children, who are closer to our ages, our third cousins.

Perhaps because our curiosity had no bounds, the conversation never lagged, and time passed rather quickly during our trip to Detroit. One of the more memorable stops we made was to have dinner in a restaurant. Harry ordered dinners for all five of us, and I could not believe the huge size of the portions we were served. We were not accustomed to consuming such enormous quantities; one dinner would have easily fed two or even three people. Among other things, I was much impressed by the enormous size of this country and its beauty.

We arrived in Detroit in the late afternoon of the next day. The Saltzmans lived in a very nice home on a beautiful tree-lined street. Rose spoke briefly to a woman who met us at the door. Shortly thereafter this person went to a car parked in front of the house, got in, and drove off. Rose explained to us that this was her housekeeper. We were somewhat taken aback that a mere housekeeper could afford to own a car. ONLY IN AMERICA!

That evening most of our cousins came to meet us. Eventually, we met them all, and it was love at first sight, if you will. They were very kind and warm people with keen senses of humor. We were teased good-naturedly about our London-acquired British accents. One could not wish for nicer people, and we hit it off right from the start.

The next day, Harry took us to see the rest of the city and the downtown area, which was teeming with shoppers. One of our first stops was at Sanders, a famous Detroit confectionery store, where he ordered some concoction called a banana split. Of course, we had no idea what that was. When the first enormous dish appeared, we thought we were going to share it. But to our amazement, three more followed. I never thought I would be able to consume the whole thing but, with "great effort," managed to do it. To this day I am not sure if I ate so much because I just forced myself, actually liked it, or simply did not want to embarrass our host.

For the time being, Nathan was staying with the Saltzmans while Bernard and I took up residence with Gertie and her husband Jack Fishman. Our first weeks in Detroit were a bit of a social whirl. All of our many cousins wanted to get better acquainted with their newfound relatives, and we were constantly being invited to different houses for dinner. We were living it up once again. Our newfound cousins in America could not have been more considerate.

One of the horrible things about being a survivor of the Holocaust is that not only have all your loved ones been murdered, but you have lost so much of your identity and family history. By the time we were liberated, my brothers and I had nothing—no photographs, no letters or other documents, not even anything to prove who we were. In fact, like so many others, my sole possession was the striped uniform I wore. When we came to our cousins in Detroit, we found what was to us a treasure trove of family photographs and letters sent to America by our grandmother. There were pictures of our grandfather, uncles, aunts, and little cousins. The most striking one was our parents' wedding photo. We could not believe how lucky we were that our American relatives had kept them all that time. Of course, they did not know who was who in the photos, and we spent hours explaining the relationships. We were amazed at the striking resemblance of the five American sisters to our mother and her three sisters. Even their Jewish names were the same.

We also found some tragic letters from my uncles Joel and Leon. Uncle Joel's calligraphy-like letter is displayed at our Holocaust Memorial Center. Written in Yiddish and German at the time of the German occupation (1939-41) when the US and Germans still maintained diplomatic relations, these letters do not mention outright all the killings and atrocities, but one can read that between the lines. They thank the American relatives for their earlier help and ask if they can send some clothes as theirs are in tatters. The letters stop around the time of Pearl Harbor, which I consider to be the most tragic event in American history.

Dear Auntie and my loving cousins,

I am writing you about our health—and it is good to hear from you.

Dear Auntie do not be angry that I did not inquire a whole summer as to the condition of your health. The reason is I am extremely busy trying to earn a living—conditions are very bad! It is so bad—we have nothing!

Dearest Auntie and dear cousins please do not be angry and do not be embarrassed, perhaps you can send me an old piece of clothing (suit). My clothes are in tatters.

I am very neglected as I cannot make new things as I am not earning anything.

The holiday is now approaching and I am ashamed to go and pray with torn and tattered attire. God should help me already that I should not have to suffer. I should only be able to write you letters of good news and not ask your help.

Write and tell me how dear Auntie's health is—also my loving cousins and their conditions.

Mother is thank God healthy. She sends her heartiest regards.

Dear cousins—I beg you—you should not forget me because I am in a very bad circumstance. With present holiday _____. God should be good. Dear Auntie should live—you should never know of sorrow and hard times, because you're keeping me alive.

I have very little work and I am appealing to you and begging, please send to my address—mail package.

I send my regards to Auntie and my heartiest regards to my cousins—also regards from my loving wife and child.

From me your devoted nephew, Joel. My address is:

Joel Schiffer
Krakow XXII
Poland

With the help of my new cousin Julius Hirschman, who worked as an accountant for a Mr. Bochnek, who was then the president of the Detroit Master Furriers Guild, I got a job with Ceresnie Brothers, a fur establishment on Dexter Avenue. A couple of months later, Nathan moved to New Jersey. He became engaged to Helen Goldberg, a survivor he had met in London. She had lost her whole family in Poland, but had found an uncle residing in New Jersey and wanted to settle near him. They were married there on July 15, 1951. I had recently purchased a brand new white 1951 Chevrolet, becoming a car owner like almost everybody else in America, and Bernard and I drove to the wedding. The Saltzmans also came for that happy event.

Early in 1952, Bernard was drafted into the American army. He became a proud GI and served in Korea, where he became a naturalized citizen of the US.

In February 1952, I met a lovely young lady named Hyla Lesser, a 1948 graduate of the University of Michigan, and we hit it off instantly. Hyla was born and raised in Detroit. Her parents, Anna and Jack Lesser, were immigrants. Jack was born in Russia and came to this country to avoid serving the Czar's army, while Anna came here as a child from Romania. A caseworker for the bureau of social aid in Detroit, Hyla loved her job and was devoted to her clients.

At least on my part, it was love at first sight. After about six weeks of courtship I proposed, but not in a conventional way. Since fishing was one of my hobbies at that time, I knew one fishing license would be valid for a spouse too, as long as it was co-signed. One evening, I asked Hyla if she would like to sign the license so we could fish together, forever. I don't recall if she hesitated or not, but she signed it. And thus, our joy and happiness began. We were married on June 19, 1952, at the Park Shelton Hotel in Detroit, with both my brothers in attendance as best men. Hyla never became a fisherperson, only a great wife, mother, friend, and confidante, and our wedding day remains the happiest occasion in my life.

We were soon blessed with two lovely and adorable children. Our first-born son, Jerry, arrived on January 8, 1954, followed by our daughter, Gail, born on July 3, 1956. We lived in a three-bedroom upstairs flat on Fullerton Street near Dexter Avenue, and our happiness and good fortune continued.

In February 1954, I opened my own fur shop on Dexter Avenue a few blocks away from Ceresnie, and we became friendly competitors. I worked very hard, sometimes seven days a week in the winter season, but I was very content because the business prospered. In 1955, I was honored and very proud to become an American citizen. It was the dream of almost a lifetime come true. I was very excited about the fact that for the first time in my life, I would be able to vote. Obtaining American citizenship afforded me that long-sought freedom of expression, not available to so many citizens of other countries and yet, regrettably, ignored by so many of those born in America. My very first vote was to retain President Eisenhower for a second term. As commander of the Allied forces, he had liberated the camps and saved my life. For that reason alone, it was incumbent upon me to retain an incumbent president in office (pardon my pun).

Normally, it takes five years to become a citizen, however, if you marry an American it takes just three years. Since Hyla was American-born, I took a ribbing from some of my friends that this was the real reason why I married her.

Bernard was now engaged and planned to get married to Sybil Weinstein in December 1957. We all had fond memories of Miriam Friedman, the widow with whom we had lived during our time in London, and had always wanted to see her again. We made arrangements for her trip to America, and she was the guest of honor at Bernard's wedding. She stayed in America for several months, alternating between Helen and Nathan's house in New Jersey and our home in Detroit. It was so grand to spend time with her (over the years we have continued to visit her in London, always being welcomed by her family like long-lost relatives).

Our children were growing, and we yearned to get a larger place. In January 1959, we happily put down a deposit on a brand new home, which was being built for us in suburban Detroit, as was the fashion for young couples then. I was beginning to live the American dream. The future looked bright.

Chapter 15

Accident

On the evening of March 23, 1959, exactly eight years after I arrived in Detroit, I planned to go out bowling, but first, I had to make a stop at my accountant's office. As I left and was about to get in my car, I was struck by a drunk driver. Waking up in a hospital a couple of days later, I knew that something terrible had happened to me. Little by little and very gently, Hyla and the doctors broke the bad news: my pelvis and left shoulder had been crushed, I had internal injuries, my right arm was in traction, my left leg had been amputated at the hip, and I could barely move. "Otherwise, nothing serious?" I asked. A little later, a nurse came in with a *Detroit Free Press* newspaper and showed us the headline, which stated, "The Nazis tried their best to kill Sam Offen, they couldn't. But what they failed in, had almost been accomplished by an American—a hit and run driver."

Weeks of healing at the hospital followed, with my beloved Hyla constantly at my side. Courageously, she masked her distress with her ever-present smile. My children were not permitted to visit, and I missed them very much. Occasionally they would come by the window and wave from below; they also threw kisses, which helped. My fur store stayed in operation (although on a limited basis since this was not the busy season) with the help of my loyal employees and some of my fellow furriers.

I received over three hundred get-well cards from friends, relatives, customers, and even total strangers who had read about my plight in the newspapers. One of my favorites was from one of my customers, who wrote, "Mr. Offen please get well soon because my fur coat needs you."

Learning of my misfortune, the man who was building our house came to visit me in the hospital. He asked if we were still planning to move to our "dream" home, which was nearing completion. After a lengthy discussion, Hyla and I decided that it would be too physically taxing for me. The builder very kindly refunded our deposit.

Eventually, I was fitted with a prosthesis and had to undergo extensive physical therapy. Perhaps because I always did more than my therapists required, I made very rapid progress and my doctors were delighted. I have adjusted so well to the prosthesis that I am often asked to talk to new wearers. Life returned to normal, and I have no regrets. It could have been much worse—I could have lost my life. So I was thankful and started a new life with my loving family. I was only thirty-seven years old.

Finally, on June 1, 1960, we moved to a new home in Southfield. A month later, on July 1, 1960, I became a full partner in a new company named Ceresnie Brothers and Offen Furs, Inc. In 1965, I was elected president of the Furriers Guild of Detroit, and in 1969 we moved Ceresnie and Offen Furs to Birmingham, in suburban Detroit.

In 1977, I was diagnosed with condro-sarcoma in my remaining leg. After several days of tests, the doctors' diagnosis was that it, too, would have to be amputated. My world collapsed. What was going to happen to my family? How would I manage? But once again, fortune rather than misfortune smiled on me. By pure coincidence, we found a maverick orthopedic surgeon, Dr. Ralph Marcove of New York's Sloan-Kettering Hospital. Dr. Marcove specialized in experimental treatments in cancer cases such as mine by removing the femur and replacing it with bone from a cadaver or some other material. My doctor explained my condition to Dr. Marcove and he agreed to accept me for an evaluation. Hyla and I flew to New York and after a lengthy examination, it was determined that my diseased femur had to be removed and replaced with a stainless steel rod. That choice was far preferable to losing my remaining leg.

Unfortunately, a hitch developed on the operating table. When my infected femur was removed, it proved to be two inches longer than the stainless steel rod that the surgeon had prepared. Since this was experimental surgery, this was the only appliance available, and he had no choice but to finish the surgery. Thus, I became two inches shorter.

I recovered fully and will forever be thankful to Dr. Marcove for saving my leg. It was a true miracle. I do not consider myself handicapped, just inconvenienced, and I don't let this stand in my way. In 1995, Dr. Marcove replaced the original steel rod in my leg (which had worn away the cartilage on my hip bone) with one made of space-age material. I am still able to pursue my previous hobbies: fishing, swimming, long-distance driving, extensive travel (Hyla and I have visited every state in the Union and every Canadian province except Newfoundland), and reading, among others. I belong to several civic and religious organizations, and still work part-time. I also enjoy a good game of poker.

Sometime in the 1980s, I was approached by the Holocaust Memorial Center (at that time located in West Bloomfield) and asked to become one of their speakers (after each tour of the center, a survivor tells the visitors his or her story). It took the management of this new institution months to persuade me that as a survivor it was my duty to speak out. I am not a trained public speaker, but it seemed important to confront a sometimes disbelieving public, if for no other reason than to memorialize those who were lost. I finally agreed to become a survivor/speaker and I have never regretted that decision. I have lectured to thousands of people over the past twenty years and have developed many friendships through this activity.

Occasionally at the conclusion of my talk, I am asked by the students to show my tattoo (or cattle brand, as I call it). Seeing this KL never fails to have a chilling effect on them.

Chapter 16

Revisiting the Past

For years, a part of me yearned to visit Poland. After all, it was my birthplace and the birthplace of my forebears, and I had spent a happy childhood there. On the other hand, it represented the worst time of my life. For a long time, I simply could not bring myself to visit a place where most of my family had perished.

Finally, in May 1985, I returned to Poland, joined by my wife Hyla, daughter Gail, son Jerry, and son in law Randy, in what has become known as the Offen Family Roots Tour. I was anxious to show my family around and be their guide.

We went first to Krakow, which, unlike other cities in Poland, was not destroyed by the Germans. I am not sure if this is because they withdrew in haste from the quickly advancing Soviet troops or they respected its historical status as the former capital of Poland. Since the city has not changed too much, it felt to me as if I had never left, and I could easily find my way around. The only noticeable difference was the unkempt condition of most buildings. Poland was still struggling economically under the Communist yoke.

Krakow still is a beautiful city, called by some the Paris of the east. Before the war, it was a vibrant, pulsating city, full of life and culture. There was an opera house, as well as several Polish and Jewish theaters. Krakow became famous for institutes of Jewish learning called *yeshivahs* as well as the famous Jagiellonian University, the second oldest in Europe (where Copernicus studied). There were also many movie theaters. I remember American movies, particularly Westerns, being very popular. Commerce flourished, and there was a thriving media. In addition to national newspapers published in Polish, there were also local papers in Polish, Yiddish, and Hebrew. As elsewhere in Poland, there was poverty, but there also existed a middle class and some very wealthy individuals, including some Jews. Of the pre-war population of two hundred thousand, some seventy thousand were Jewish.

Presently, sad to say, there are fewer than two hundred Jews, mainly older ones, left in Krakow. There are about a half dozen Jewish-style restaurants and shops selling Judaica; there are also a few klezmer bands, catering mainly to tourists. Regrettably, none of the proprietors are Jewish. Krakow is about an hour's drive from Auschwitz, thus it is a usual stop for people wishing to visit the site of the worst Jewish tragedy. Interestingly, young Polish people, who perhaps have never met a Jewish person, are now interested in the lost Jewish culture and are patronizing these so-called Jewish establishments.

While we were in Krakow, I read the local paper and found a recipe for carp prepared "Jewish style"—a dish I remembered from my childhood. Onions and carrots in a sweet jellied broth accompany the specially raised carp in this traditional dish. I translated the recipe for my family, reading the first line as: "First, you kill the fish." My children laughed and said "Gross." Perhaps they thought fish came out of the water already formed into fish sticks!

One of the first places we visited was the three-story apartment house where I lived as a child, built at the turn of the century and still standing. Because I was driving a brand new, foreign, nine-passenger minibus, we were very noticeable. Unlike years ago when multitudes of Jewish children, including me, were at play in the streets, we saw very few children. I parked the vehicle and we went straight to our old apartment on the ground floor and knocked. A lady opened the door only partially and asked what we wanted. I still speak fluent Polish, so I explained that I was born in this apartment many years ago and would like to show it to my American-born family. She hesitated, giving all kinds of excuses, finally saying that she was busy cooking dinner for her husband who would be coming home from work soon. I pleaded with her to let us in for just a couple of minutes. Reluctantly, she agreed but told us to hurry. We looked around and took a couple of pictures. The apartment looked almost the same except for the contemporary appliances and different furnishings. I had a lump in my throat, looking around, trying to reconstruct my childhood, and visualizing the long-gone members of my family moving about the place, keeping busy at different tasks. It was a very traumatic episode, but rewarding in the sense that my accompanying family was able to experience my long-ago, happy past before tragedy struck.

To better understand the reluctance of the Polish lady to let us in the apartment, one has to appreciate the mentality of a lot of Polish people in the post-war situation. They feared that surviving Jews would come back to claim their properties. There were circumstances when Jews were beaten up and even killed for trying to repossess their belongings. The attitude of some Poles was "too bad the Nazis did not kill the rest of you." Yet, one has to admit there were other circumstances when properties and other valuables, hidden by the Poles from the Nazis, were gladly returned to the survivors.

We also visited my school, named after a Polish-American Revolutionary war hero, Thadeusz Kosciuszko, which was in a beautiful brick building along the Vistula River. He was also known as "friend of the Jews." In one of the many synagogues, there was a plaque with his quote stating "When humanity is at stake, Jews know how to shed their blood." It still serves as a school. Other than one survivor I met at Shabbat services, I met no one I knew before the war, not even a former Polish schoolmate. How sad.

We even ate at Pod Wierzynek, the historic restaurant, which my father had once supplied with toothpicks and which I never dreamed I would set foot in as a customer. It was by far the best dinner we had in all of our time in Poland.

The next visits were very depressing, yet so necessary. We went to Auschwitz, where my father was killed, and Belzec and Majdanek, where my mother and sister were killed. We lit *yahrzeit* (memorial) candles, said Kaddish, cried a lot, hugged and consoled each other, reflecting collectively on our great and irreplaceable loss. Because so many of my family was killed, my own children were deprived of having grandparents, aunts, uncles and cousins. We realized the enormity of our loss.

I had an interesting and and eye-opening, but not totally unexpected, experience at Auschwitz. The Communist government in power at that time did not specifically differentiate between Jews and Poles as victims. We were all lumped in the category of Polish citizen. I guess it suited their anti-Semitic propaganda purposes. Since we had a private English-speaking guide, I broke away and went to listen to a Polish teacher talking to his students next to a gallows with multiple ropes hanging down. My suspicion was confirmed. All the victims were cited only as Polish citizens; it was never mentioned that the majority were Jews.

We also visited Plaszow, where nothing remains of that large concentration camp with the exception of a crumbling stone monument erected by the Jewish community of Krakow in this now peaceful pasture. It bears the following inscription in both Polish and Yiddish:

> In this place, in the years 1943–1945, tens of thousands of Jews from Poland and Hungary were murdered and their remains cremated. We do not know the names of the murdered ones, but we do know that they were Jews. In this place, human speech does not have words to describe the incredible bestiality, suffering, and cruelty. But we do know that it was committed under Hitlerism.
>
> In memory of those whose last screams exist as silence in this Plaszow cemetery, and who were murdered under the Fascist pogroms.

Reading this inscription brought back a memory. In 1944, as inmates at Plaszow, my brothers and I had seen large groups of well-dressed people (not undernourished like us) marching under heavy Nazi guard toward this execution place, followed by the sound of machine-gun fire. Only later did we find out that those people were Hungarian Jews.

Before the war, we used to play soccer nearby. Never in our wildest dreams did we imagine that so many of us would become victims of the Nazi barbarians and wind up dead in those ravines. How could we?

In Majdanek, authorities had erected a large memorial in the shape of an urn. The urn contains ashes and small bone fragments, perhaps those of my loved ones, with an inscription in Polish which translates as "Let our fate forever be a warning to all humanity." It is a very poignant description.

Another memorable excursion was to the Wieliczka salt mine, located about seven or eight miles east of Krakow, where my brother Nathan and I were slave laborers for several weeks. This mine has been in constant operation for hundreds of years, and through the years, in a section of the mine that forms a large hall, Polish artists have carved a chapel, religious figures, chandeliers, and other priceless artifacts out of the rock salt. UNESCO has declared the mine a historic area, but because of water seepage, the great hall is in danger and UNESCO is funding its preservation.

I wanted to show my family this place of horror, which had long been so vivid in my mind, but I was advised by the English-speaking guide that it would be next to impossible for me to navigate the low, narrow, and uneven corridors. Reluctantly, I stayed above, while my family boarded a narrow lift and rode down to the bowels of the mine. Some time later they came up and informed me that they had told the guide of my experiences there.

The guide must have telephoned the mine management to tell them about my travails. Soon I was greeted by a rather large number of officials and miners who had worked in the mine during the time I was there. Some of them may have been among those who gave my brother and me extra food. They all shook my hand and embraced me. Apparently, I was the first survivor of that ordeal who had ever returned for a visit. They had a hard time believing that anyone actually survived. We reminisced about those difficult times and I expressed my heartfelt gratitude for their extraordinary gift of life-saving food and other help. It was quite an experience to meet these miners more than forty years later.

At the conclusion of our visit, I received a special treat. We descended via a VIP elevator to the magnificent rock-salt hall so painstakingly created by those Polish artists, so I was able to see their work after all.

Our last stop in Krakow was in the ghetto, now renamed "Ghetto Hero's Square." This was a very important square because it was where so many executions and deportations took place. From this cursed location, thousands of Jews were transported to death camp. There existed a drug store on the square, the only one allowed in the ghetto, owned and operated by a Polish gentile. His name was Mr. Tadeusz Pankiewicz, and it existed for many years and for some unknown reasons, the Germans allowed it to operate. Mr. Pankiewicz was able to occasionally help some ghetto inmates with food, medicine, etc. He was also able to smuggle out of the ghetto some valuable information to the free world and was the only non-Jewish witness of the Nazi atrocities. This former drugstore is currently a museum housing photographs taken by the Germans, recovered from their archives. Mr. Pankiewicz is still alive and lives in Krakow. He was honored for his humanitarian deeds by all kinds of international organizations, including the Yad Vashem in Israel, as a righteous gentile. The pharmacy's name was "Under the Eagle."

Another interesting experience happened in Warsaw, where the Communist government of the time supported a Yiddish theater named after a famous pre-war Yiddish actress named Ida Kaminka. Perhaps their goal was to attract more Jewish tourists. One evening Hyla and I attended a Sholom Aleichem play in Yiddish at this theater. There were some other Americans present, but the audience mostly consisted of young Polish people who were able to understand what was going on by wearing earphones through which they heard an instantaneous translation from Yiddish to Polish. We loved the performance and also appreciated the fact that so many young Polish people were interested. The sad fact was that, although their Yiddish was perfect, all the actors were Polish. Still, I was elated that some semblance of Yiddish culture was being upheld in the country of my birth.

After the war, some Jewish survivors returned to Poland in search of their lost families. Others came out of hiding, having been living in secret in churches, on farms, and in private homes, protected by Polish citizens who were decent, caring human beings who risked their own lives to help Jews. For different reasons, some of these survivors married Catholic spouses. Most hid those facts from their descendants in fear of anti-Semitism. Later on, in their advanced years, some confessed their origins to their children or grandchildren. Perhaps some of those descendants were in the audience at that Jewish theater also. (Before and after Communism fell in Eastern Europe, the heirs of the Lauder cosmetic company have made many attempts to bring those offspring back to Judaism. The Lauder Foundation organizes summer camps for children, sets up Jewish cultural events, and brings rabbis and other teachers in to teach about Judaism. What a noble cause!)

When we left the theater it was late at night and no taxi would stop to take us to our hotel. We went to the streetcar stop, which was almost deserted, except for one couple. I inquired in Polish about the fare. The man informed me that only tokens could be used, but no currency. Since I did not know the procedure, he assumed I was from out of town and asked where I came from.

Without a moment's hesitation, I answered that I was from Krakow. I thought so, he replied. There had always been a sort of linguistic rivalry in Poland between Warsaw and Krakow. I proceeded to explain that although I was born in Krakow, I had not been there in over forty years and that I was an American and so was my wife, Hyla. He was impressed and said he liked Americans. Just then the streetcar arrived and we all boarded. We sat down and had a nice conversation, with me translating everything for Hyla. He informed me that although the Polish people regard Americans as friends, they have never forgiven President Roosevelt for his almost traitorous act in abandoning them to the Soviet political sphere. Most Poles abhor Communism, he assured me.

As we approached our stop, he embraced me and asked, "How come you did not teach your wife to speak Polish?" Since the subject of why I had left Poland hadn't surfaced, I doubt he suspected I was Jewish.

Warsaw was almost totally leveled by the Germans in August of 1944. As the Soviet army advanced toward the German-occupied city, the residents, thinking that help was near, staged an uprising. But Stalin betrayed the Poles. He halted his armies just short of Warsaw on the eastern side of the Vistula River. Though brave, the Poles were no match for the German army and were massacred by the tens of thousands. Weeks later, the Soviets marched in as "liberators." After the war, slowly, but very meticulously, workers and artisans rebuilt the old town, with its castle, palaces, and other historic places, to pre-war conditions.

The last camp we visited in Europe was Mauthausen in Austria, where I was liberated. To this day, Austria falsely claims that the country itself was a victim of Hitler and denies its complicity in Nazi crimes, consequently refusing to pay well-deserved compensation to the real victims. Statistics show that, per capita, there were more Austrian Nazis than German ones. Perish the thought. Even the infamous and brutal commander of the Plaszow camp, Amon Goeth, was from Vienna.

Therefore, for a long time, the Austrians refused to let Mauthausen become a sort of museum, which is what has generally happened to camps in other countries. Finally, bowing to world pressure they opened the camp up, but they "prettified" it by planting lawns and flowers in front of the barracks and on the camp square. During my detention I would have been amazed to see flowers—there was only deep mud, dust, and stones—and I was so hungry that if the grass or flowers had been there at that time, I would have devoured them. In my wildest dreams I did not expect to survive this camp, much less to become a visitor after forty years. For a moment I regretted returning to this place of death, yet something compelled me. I wanted to forget the hellish place where I almost perished. I was here with my family and wanted my children to realize that without remembering, there can be no future and a holocaust might reoccur. This visit to

Mauthausen is akin of a personal triumph and bittersweet victory over the Nazis. This is a place where I survived against all odds and where I was reborn.

Our bestial camp commander, Franz Zalreis, was caught by the prisoners after liberation and held for the American army. The official note in the camp shortly afterwards stated that he died from the wounds suffered while trying to escape.

Before leaving, I said Kaddish, the prayer for the dead, for all those who died so needlessly just days prior to liberation.

*****

Whenever I talk about my experiences during the war, I am frequently asked, why did we not resist the Nazis? First of all, when you are starving, your foremost thought is your next slice of bread. Secondly, we had only our bare hands to fight an overwhelmingly strong enemy, something that our weakened condition made even more impossible.

However, there were instances of resistance in some of the camps and ghettos. In Krakow, a group of young people assassinated some high-ranking SS officers as they ate in one of their favorite restaurants, called Cyganerja. Unfortunately, they were all caught and executed.

The most famous uprising, of course, occurred in the Warsaw Ghetto in 1943. There, several dozen desperate individuals, knowing they were about to be transported to the gas chambers at Treblinka, decided to make a last stand. With a small number of handguns smuggled in from outside the ghetto, under the leadership of Mordechi Anielewicz, these few bravely resisted the mighty German army. The battle lasted a whole month. In the end, most of those heroes and heroines were killed, but a few managed to save themselves at the end of the battle by escaping through the sewers.

Jews also fought the Nazis in the forests of eastern Poland and as part of the partisan forces in the western Ukraine. There they derailed German military trains and committed all sorts of sabotage, thus helping the Allied cause. Many of these Jews perished, not only at the hands of the Germans, but also at those of their non-Jewish "comrades in arms." It seems inconceivable to me that even while fighting a cruel common enemy in dire conditions, some people could not forget the old anti-Semitic hatred.

Chapter 17

Finding Donald Montgomery, My Liberator

Ever since I arrived in America, it was my desire to meet one of the GIs in the platoon of fifteen or twenty soldiers that liberated me from certain death at Mauthausen-Gusen. I tried very hard, but my search seemed to be futile. Around 1992, by sheer luck, my brother Nathan met a retired army captain from New Jersey who had served in Europe during World War II. We exchanged some information, and to my amazement he told me that one of the units of his Eleventh Armored Division ("The Thunderbolts") had liberated Mauthausen, but he did not know which one. Since he was an officer in their civilian association, he knew a lot about the division.

Formed in 1943, the Eleventh Armored Division consisted mostly of men from the northeastern part of the United States but also contained a fair contingent of men from the midwest. The retired captain also told me that in 1993, which would be the fiftieth anniversary of their formation, they were going to honor the memory of their fallen comrades by issuing a commemorative book. Since we had been liberated by that division, the captain asked if Nathan and I would like to write a letter for the book's introduction. Our letter concluded with the following:

> *Eventually, we emigrated to the USA and proudly became American citizens, an honor we will cherish forever. Now, forty-five years later, a lot of changes have occurred. History has been re-written, alliances have changed, and the whole world seems different. Millions of innocent people were killed by the Nazis. There were tens of thousands*

of Nazi oppressors and executioners who personally took part in humanity's most cruel period, ever. Other than the Nuremberg trials, and a few individual trials, how many of them ever came to justice?

Even now, there are some fascist organizations claiming that the Holocaust never happened, and that Jews invented all the horror stories. Thank God, you were there to see the gas chambers, the crematoria, and the victims. Therefore, you are our best eyewitnesses and can refute their claim. To you, our dear liberators of the Eleventh Armored Division, we want to extend our most grateful thanks for saving our lives and thousands of others. It was just in time, for had you arrived a few days later, we would have surely perished.

Please accept this letter of thanks from two very fortunate and extremely grateful survivors.

HE WHO SAVES ONE LIFE IS AS IF HE WOULD SAVE THE ENTIRE WORLD.

> *Talmud*
> *Tractate Sanhedrin*
> *Page 37A*

One day in October 1993, I received a package from the Eleventh Division containing that book. Eagerly, I opened it. It contained pictures and biographies of GIs. Sadly, many of them had been killed in action, but thankfully, a fair number were still around, dispersed all over the country. I scanned the text and eventually found a GI who had liberated Mauthausen and who was living in Michigan not more than twenty miles from me. Almost a neighbor. His name was Donald R. Montgomery. I called information to get his phone number and dialed. A man answered the phone and my heart started beating faster.

"Are you Mr. Donald Montgomery?"

"Yes."

"Were you with the Eleventh Armored Division?"

"Yes."

"Were you with the 575th Anti-Aircraft Artillery that liberated Mauthausen?"

"Yes."

I proceeded to tell him my name (which of course meant nothing to him) and that I was one of those walking skeletons he and his buddies had rescued. There was a long pause on his end of the line, then, "Well, I'll be darned. I never expected any of you would make it."

We arranged to meet the next day for lunch. We embraced, cried, and exchanged stories. Don hails from the Pontiac area of Michigan and joined the army right after graduating from high school. Decorated for his army service, he felt lucky to survive when so many of his comrades did not. We celebrated with some martinis and arranged to meet with our spouses soon thereafter.

When I related that story to Rabbi Charles Rosenzveig, the founder of the Holocaust Memorial Center (the first such center in the US), he suggested that I invite Don to my next scheduled lecture at the HMC and that we both bring along our spouses.

When the scheduled day arrived, I gave my lecture, then asked Don, who is a very modest gentleman and never speaks about his experiences, if he would like to address the students.

Reluctantly he stood up and with tears in his eyes started to tell about the liberation from his vantage point, so different from my own. He remembered the survivors' appearance, "absolute skin and bones, large eyes and blue-and-gray-striped uniforms," and the piles of bodies stacked like cordwood on the ground. He concluded his story, "If I can do something to further the remembrance of the Holocaust, that's the least I can do. Even today, it wouldn't take much to start all over again."

He then pulled out of his wallet a yellowed photo and showed it to the audience. It depicted piles of bodies with a note written on the back: "Dad, you will never believe what you'll see in this pic-ture, which I took today, May 5, 1945."

Don Montgomery had sent this photo to his dad and then forgot-ten all about it. As fate would have it, Don's dad had passed away just a few months before our meeting. He went through his father's personal mementos and found that photo. After showing it to our audience, he donated it to the Holocaust Memorial Center.

Another surprise that day was that the media, having been alert-ed to our meeting by Rabbi Rosenzveig, showed up to listen to my talk. The next day's headline in the October 21, 1993 *Detroit News* proclaimed "Holocaust: Survivor, Liberator reunited after 48 years." This was followed by stories in other media and sever-al TV interviews.

Because of that publicity, another American GI, Dick LaLone, came forward. He and Don had been childhood friends but had lost touch with each other. They both joined the army but served in dif-ferent units. One day toward the end of the war, during an air raid, they found themselves together in a ditch for a brief moment, but again went separate ways. The above news story reunited them! (By coincidence, Dick LaLone's engineering battalion arrived in Mauthausen a few days after Don's division left. They brought bulldozers to dig the mass graves necessary for all the bodies.)

On May 5, 1995, together with my family, I celebrated the fifti-eth anniversary of my liberation with a party, held in a lakeside restaurant near a marina full of boats, which I love. Don and his wife Dorothy were our guests of honor. The media picked up this story, too, and Don deserved every word of praise that followed.

The six of us—the Offens, the Montgomerys, and the LaLones (including Dick's wife Betty)—became good friends. Every May 5, I get a very nice birthday card from Don, claiming it's my *new* birthday, the day I was re-born. Humbly, I accept it, for had it not been for Don, the American army, and its government, I would not be here today.

And so after a long forty-eight years, I was finally able to express my heartfelt gratitude to America, by saying thank you to a most humble human being, Donald R. Montgomery. Don's and Dick's stories have been videotaped and are available for viewing at the Holocaust Memorial Center.

To Donald Montgomery—

A courageous American GI, a very modest and unassuming man, who, not unlike the "Rescuers," is my hero.

He and other brave Americans personally liberated me from certain annihilation at the hands of the German Nazis, at the Mauthausen extermination camp.

His timely arrival with the 775th Anti-Aircraft Artillery on May 5, 1945, was just in the nick of time! Had he arrived just a few days later, I would not be alive today.

Thanks to you, Don, I was able to start a new life here in America. My whole family and I are eternally grateful to you.

Sam Offen
November 14, 1993

This was the inscription on the book I presented to Don.

Chapter 18

The Rest of the Story

Although by the end of the 1990s, Bernard, Nathan, and I had each visited Poland with our families, we had always done so separately. In August 2001, we had our first reunion together in Poland. Bernard, who spends the summers in Krakow and winters in California lecturing on the Holocaust and sometimes guiding tour groups to Auschwitz, Plaszow, and the ghetto, was our guide. He is perhaps the only survivor and eyewitness of these three places of the Nazi hell who made it his life's mission to guide tourists from around the globe. He also lectures to Polish people, mainly students, in Polish, now totaling almost two thousand people. In addition, he produced a trilogy of documentary films and tapes: *The Work, My Hometown Concentration Camp, and Process b. 7815* (his Auschwitz number).

In 2001, my brother Nathan and I and our wives traveled to Poland once again to meet with Bernard. It was our first meeting in Poland since liberation and we wanted to visit the Belzec camp together. We drove for about five hours from Krakow east almost to the Ukrainian border, through many villages, small towns, and forests. There was much silence between us. I kept wondering how such a horrendous event could have come about. I dreaded getting there. I was afraid, once there, that my fears would never stop for my beloved mother and sister and my people so brutally murdered by the German Nazis and their henchmen. And yet I knew that I had to go there to have closure and peace! The former camp was located close to the village of Belzec and a caretaker opened the gate for us. Inside the enclosure we saw a monument at which we lit a memorial candle and said Kaddish. Further away, we saw numerous, enormous mass graves of the ashes that were gathered. We did not stay long; we were shivering, not only because of the rain. Much more silence followed on the return trip and to this day, we are still affected by the memory of that place. My silence was only verbal, but within my heart and shallow breath there was an overpowering anger, depression, and a river of tears. Yet, seeing my wife and loving family brought me back to the decision to live on, to keep witnessing and to keep a positive view for life and future. Despite all that transpired for me I have had three lives—I was born free, I lived in hell, and now, I am living in paradise.

Many years after liberation, I found out that the trains that mother and sister were on in the deportation from the Krakow ghetto were sent to Belzec extermination camp. The camp existed for less than one year and then it was destroyed. During its existence, over six hundred thousand Jews were murdered there. On arrival, they were kept in the cattle cars until they were ready for the next murder operation. Upon opening of the train door, they were ordered to undress for a shower. They were shooting people all around to create fear and hurry people. Then they were driven into an enclosure which was narrow and low. When they emerged into a room, they were inside the gas chamber. The doors were quickly shut tight and an enormous engine was started from which the exhaust fumes were pumped into a chamber. Sometimes the engine would stop and could not be restarted for a time in the middle of the gassing process. It took a long time to die. Afterward, the bodies were dragged and burned on specially elevated open pits on rails; the bones were crushed and dumped in forest pits.

Since the fall of Communism and the advent of Poland's democratic government, Krakow has grown from a pre-war population of just over two hundred thousand to seven hundred thousand. The old part of town is still as charming as ever. The main growth is in the suburbs. You will find blocks and blocks of tall apartment houses and giant supermarkets, mostly owned by large European concerns.

Consequently, there is an abundance of both domestic and foreign goods, and a sizable middle class. Poland has voted to join the European Union.

Since they cannot yet effectively compete with the colossal European companies, Poland's export trade is lopsided and that in turn has created rampant unemployment. The three-story apartment house we lived in before the war is now a commercial property on the ground floor. There are traffic jams, too. These problems are prevalent in all large cities in Poland.

But the changes in Poland, while interesting, were not the sole reason we wanted to visit. The main purpose of our reunion was that we wanted to see together all those places of horror where our loved ones were so brutally annihilated by the Nazis. As we expected, that proved to be the most traumatic experience of our time in Poland. Most of the camps are in poor physical condition and need constant repairs. The Polish authorities, themselves short of funds, do make some contributions for the upkeep. The Germans and other Europeans help out also. But the bulk of the money comes from Jewish organizations in the US, with Holocaust survivors' participation. Nature is taking its course. Regrettably, there will be fewer and fewer of us to continue in this noble cause of remembrance.

Quite by chance on my 1985 trip to Poland I was able to obtain information on the birthdates of my various family members. After attending Sabbath services in the one remaining place of worship in Krakow, the three-hundred-year-old Remuh *shul*, I met a fellow survivor who helped me obtain copies of their birth certificates as well as my parents' marriage license.

Chapter 19

The Paper Clip Story Participation

In the summer of 1998, David Smith, the deputy principal and football coach at a middle school in Whitwell, Tennessee, attended a teachers' seminar in Chattanooga and heard a Holocaust survivor speak. Whitwell is a small town with a population of under two thousand, most of whom are Christians, located in a mountain valley about thirty miles west of Chattanooga. Mr. Smith was looking for some way to teach his students about hatred and intolerance, and hearing the Holocaust survivor speak gave him an idea: why not offer a voluntary course that would teach students about the Holocaust?

He pitched his proposal to the school's principal, Linda Hooper. She called a meeting for parents. Some questioned the wisdom of exposing their children to such horrific material, but relented after Ms. Hooper assured them she would allow her own child to attend this class. Thus, it became a town project.

Mr. Smith taught the class. The first year they read such works as *Anne Frank: The Diary of a Young Girl*, *I Have Lived a Thousand Years: Growing up in the Holocaust* by Livia Jackson,and *Kingdom of Auschwitz* by Otto Friedrich. They saw *Schindler's List* and other Shoah films. Most of the time, Smith read aloud to the students, because many of Whitwell's students are poor and can't afford to purchase individual books for their classes.

After learning about the enormity of the Nazi crimes, the students decided they would like to commemorate the six million who died in the Holocaust, but did not know how to do so. One of the students came up with the idea of collecting six million paper clips. Why paper clips? He had read somewhere that during World War II, many people in occupied Norway wore them on their lapels to protest Nazi race policies (the paper clip was invented in 1899 by a Norwegian, Johan Vaaler).

Thus, the Holocaust Paper Clip project began. A German couple, Dagmar and Peter Schroeder, White House correspondents for several German and Austrian newspapers, learned about this worthwhile project and put the information on the internet.

The response was overwhelming. Within a short period of time, the students received millions of paper clips from the United States and all over the world, including some from then-President Bill Clinton and Vice President Al Gore, who is from Tennessee. I learned of the project in the fall of 2001, when I read a small article about it in *Hadassah* magazine. I called David Smith to find out more, and he invited my wife Hyla and me to visit. In February 2002, on our way to Florida, we stopped at Whitwell, where we were greeted by Smith and all the teachers with real southern hospitality.

Among other things, we learned that, prior to their special project, none of the students, and very few of the townspeople, had ever encountered a Jew. The students and teachers assembled in the auditorium, and I talked to them about my Holocaust experiences. Questions and answers followed. We then stepped outside. In front of the building, I saw a cattle car of the kind used to transport Jews to death or concentration camps. Inside the car, there were more than *fifteen million* paper clips! The students' next goal was to collect more clips for a total of 18 million—the letter *chai* stands for eighteen and is also the Hebrew symbol for life.

Just before leaving, we asked about the origin of the cattle car (which the Schroeders had been instrumental in obtaining). To my shock, we found it came from Krakow. It was chilling to realize that members of my family, friends, or even *I* might have been transported in this very car! As a postscript, a school from Jasper, a nearby town, called me because they wanted more information to help them write a play about the Holocaust. A few months later, we received a videotape from the school. When we viewed the tape we were surprised and honored to find that the play was dedicated to Hyla and Sam Offen.

*****

There was a time in my life when I was at the mercy of the Nazis, whose cruel ideology sought to destroy not just me but an entire people. Somehow I survived and now I take comfort in my greatest act of defiance—the creation of a family, which means that my name (and that of my beloved parents) will be perpetuated. Since that family is so important to me, here's a bit about them.

Our daughter, Gail Marian, is named after my mother and sister. She graduated from the University of Michigan as an English major and is employed in an advertising agency in the capacity of creative director and senior vice president. She is married to Dr. Randy Samuels, who graduated from Michigan State and the University of Detroit Dental School. Our son, Jerry Alan, is named after my Dad and Hyla's uncle. He graduated from Michigan State University as an engineer and is employed in the automotive industry. He is married to Karen, also a Michigan State University graduate who is a computer support specialist. During the darkest moments of my life I thought I would never become a husband, much less a father. To have had the privilege of creating these two wonderful children means that I was ultimately able to snatch victory away from the Nazis.

Hyla's family owned a summer cottage on a lake about forty miles from Detroit. It was built by Hyla's parents in the 1930s. Our children, like their cousins, spent their happiest summers there. My wife's brothers, Mort and Bob, and their wives (both named Elaine) also would spend much of the summer there with their children. I used to drive there almost daily after work from our house in Southfield. It's hard to believe so many people could cram into such a small space (and only one bathroom!).

Happily, we now have four generations in our extended family, the latest one arriving in summer of 2003. Because of changing circumstances we are now spending only weekends at "the cottage." The Lesser family bought the cottage next door in the 1970s as their family grew larger. On any given Sunday, we have between fifteen and twenty-five family members and friends present for dinner. Because of our constant contact, we are a very close and loving family, envied by many. We always had, and still have, great and memorable good times there, fostering relationships that no money could buy. It is our family's priceless compound.

The foremost occasion recently celebrated was our golden wedding anniversary in June 2002. Our children Gail, Randy, Karen, and Jerry, hosted a sumptuous party for us in one of the most historic restaurants in Detroit. It was attended by almost fifty members of both Hyla's and my families and of course, my brothers Nathan and Bernard and their companions. It was an affair to remember. I am a very lucky man. To be surrounded by friends and family is the greatest gift, and one that I could not have imagined sixty years ago.

Afterword

istory's most tragic event ever occurred during the Nazi Holocaust when six million Jewish people, including one and one half million children, perished from the face of this earth. It is an incomprehensible figure. The state of Michigan where I reside consists of over nine million people—imagine if two-thirds of its residents were wiped out. The sad truth is that this is precisely what happened to us. Murdering one and one half million children was heart-wrenching. Had they survived, we might have a much better world today.

By 1942 the Nazis had already murdered hundreds of thousands or perhaps millions of Jews by different methods including those in their victorious conquests in the Soviet territory. The Allies knew about those atrocities, but did not lift a finger. This had emboldened the Germans and, in 1942, the highest SS Nazis met in a villa at Wansee, outside of Berlin, and decreed officially that the rest of the Jews under their brutal yoke had to be dealt with and thus liquidated. Jews ceased to have the right to live.

The question most often asked by my audiences is, how did you survive? My answer inevitably is that I cannot attribute it to any one cause. Perhaps I was in the right place at the right time, perhaps providence intervened and it was my destiny to survive and tell the world about the Nazis' cruelty. I never gave up hope.

Even after all these years I have occasional nightmares. I dream about my past and yell and scream and Hyla has to shake me to reality. But life goes on, although the pain in my heart never goes away.

I am also frequently asked if I can ever forgive the Nazis. My answer is that only those who were so brutally murdered can forgive. For me to do so would be a betrayal of my loving family and all those others lost to history through the Holocaust.

But then there is the question of the thousands of Nazi officers who personally perpetrated all the suffering and killings on their innocent victims and got away with it.

In 1946, at the Nuremberg trials, several very high-ranking Nazis were found guilty of crimes against humanity. Deplorably, only a miniscule number of lower-ranking criminals ever were brought to justice. What disturbs me most is the fact that many of them immigrated to this country illegally, falsifying their war record on the visa application. An unspecified number continue to live among us. They are "exemplary" citizens, their neighbors not knowing of their brutal past.

About twenty years ago the Special Investigations Office of the Justice Department in Washington, DC made a concerted effort to find these war criminals. The Justice Department brought to trial a number of camp guards who had been discovered living in the US and obtained many convictions, but very few of these individuals were ever deported, and thus eluded justice. Because of their advanced years, they will not have to answer for their heinous crimes, ever!

I am not looking for revenge, and am realistic enough to realize that at this point, even if some judgments were carried out, *justice* would be an illusion. These men have been able to live their lives, something my family was denied. It is bitter medicine to know that the most unimaginable human suffering in history will remain basically unpunished.

When I speak at the Holocaust Memorial Center or at other venues my listeners are usually high school and university students, and I try to impress upon them that as our future leaders, it is important that they understand what happened in the Holocaust. I remind them that in addition to Jews, millions of Christian civilians were killed by the Nazis—for all kinds of "reasons." Among them were German-born Christians who were either physically or mentally disabled, gypsies, gays, and political prisoners. The Polish intelligentsia and Catholic priests, in particular, were decimated by the Nazis. If, God forbid, a mad dictator were to take control of *our* beloved country, who knows what could happen.

I hope that listening to a surviving eyewitness will bring home the story in a way that reading about this sad history in a book never could. I tell them that we must never fail to exercise our democratic values and fight injustice, bigotry, and hatred, for the sake of all humanity. This is our only hope to prevent other genocides. In the end, we have to be our brothers' keepers. I always was an optimist, and I still believe in the basic goodness of humanity.

One of my proudest moments occurred on April 11, 1983, while attending the first-ever gathering of Holocaust survivors in Washington, DC. We were addressed by President Ronald Reagan with these words:

> *Tonight we stand together to give thanks to America for providing freedom and liberty and, for many here tonight, a second home and a second life.*
>
> *The opportunity to join with you this evening as a representative of the people of the United States will be for me a cherished memory. I am proud to accept your thanks on behalf of our fellow Americans and also to express our gratitude to you for choosing America, for being the good citizens that you are, and for reminding us of how important it is to remain true to our ideals as individuals and as a nation.*

His words still ring loud and clear today.

God Bless America!

Background Notes

We never were able to retrieve my mother's needlepoint picture of Moses. After the war, my brothers and I searched futilely for Mr. Cieslik. Years later we found out he had gotten married and moved to Chicago. By the time we discovered this, he had passed away and his wife had Alzheimer's. We were able to contact several of his children, who were still living in Poland, but they, having been only children during the war, knew nothing of our mother's precious legacy. Thus, the last connection to our pre-war family life was irretrievably lost.

In 2002, another document pertaining to my family came to light. The Austrians, like their German counterparts, are known as immaculate record keepers. My brother Bernard, through his contacts in Austria and after months of searching, was able to obtain a copy of our father's Austrian Army military record. This detailed history names the various battles in which he fought, the illnesses and injuries he incurred, his hospital stays, and gives his pay records as a soldier in World War I. Interestingly, it states that most Jews served in engineering battalions, building temporary bridges and fortifications, because they refused to fight on the Sabbath.

On February 20, 2005 the New Cracow Friendship Society, an organization of Holocaust survivors from Krakow and its vicinity, was honored by Steven Spielberg at a banquet at the Fontainbleau Hotel in Miami Beach. He became famous for making and producing the movie *Schindler's List*. It featured a German who single-handedly saved over twelve hundred Jews from almost certain death. The over six hundred of us present celebrated and commemorated our miraculous survival.

Many present were from different parts of the country and we all had a great and memorable time. My brothers and I attended with our significant others. A good number of Schindler survivors were present too. Mr. Spielberg could not attend—he addressed us via video.

Since I know a number of these survivors, some of whom were my childhood friends or schoolmates, we rejoiced, cried, and said our farewells. Sadly, this might have been our last gathering of this magnitude.

A Daughter's Tribute

As difficult as this book is to read, I know it was even harder for my father to write. For years, my father refused to talk about his Holocaust experiences. Some nights I heard the cries from his terrible dreams. But his need to tell his story to the world finally overcame him, and now he shares it with people all over the country.

To return to Poland with my father and family was overwhelming. Standing by my father's side at camps like Auschwitz, Belzec and Mauthausen where his family was murdered was, frankly, the lowest point in my life. But it was important for my father to be surrounded by the living while mourning the dead. To say Kaddish, to say goodbye. This final chapter was more than a catharsis—it made him realize that the world needs to keep being reminded of the horror. And so began this book.

Most of all, my father is an optimist. Cheerful, very funny, and always looking for the good in people. He has endured so much pain, yet every day looks at the world with a positive eye. They say every Holocaust survivor has a story to tell. And to tell it and remain an optimist, well, that is truly the most amazing story of all.

Gail Offen

Responses from Student and Educator Attendees of Sam Offen's Speaking Engagements

Dear Mr. Offen,

. . . I promise you I will never forget the history you have shown to me, the lifetime you have shared with me, or the memories you have given me. I will never forget what you have taught me.

Sincerely,

Cameron W.

Dear Mr. Offen,

Thank you for giving so much of yourself to so many. Our students have learned a great deal of history and humanity from you. Mr. Offen, you truly are an inspiration to all of us here.

Linda H.

Dear Sam,

The minute the kids boarded the bus to return home, they wanted to talk about all they had heard. Their conversation focused on the stories you told and their intense admiration for your ability to endure all you that did. Survival strategies are important insights for teenagers who sometimes feel that the violence they see today is constant and, unfortunately, normal. Youth who hear stories from survivors of violence develop images of hopefulness. Thank you!

Sincerely yours,

Marty D.

Dear Mr. Offen,

. . . You are such an inspiration to me because you have had to deal with so much, and yet you never cease to see the good in everyone and all around you. I hold immense honor to your name and I am forever grateful for the time you have spent explaining memories of your personal Holocaust to young people. Not only did you educate me about this utterly terrible event, you taught me how to be full of life and optimism. I will no longer look at a 'simple' pleasure such as taking a stroll as if it is nothing. I thank you for that. You will never be forgotten in my mind.

Sincerely,

Evelyn Marie C.

Dear Mr. Offen,

Thank you so much for coming to share your story with our high school. As always, you made a deep impression on the students.

Sincerely,

Judy D.

Dear Mr. Offen,

I sincerely do hope that your bravery, stability, skill, wisdom, and confidence rub off on me. Thank you very much for coming in to talk with us.

Won-Woo L.

Dear Mr. Offen,

. . . God really does want you to stay on Earth to teach people not to take life for granted, which is why he saved you from death so many times. We were so fortunate to have you visit, you inspired us all. Thank you for coming to speak to us Mr. Offen. You have a heart of gold.

Sincerely,

Blythe P.

Dear Mr. Offen,

Since you came to our school, I have prayed almost every day that nothing like the Holocaust will ever happen again. Even if you help one person see the horror of the Holocaust it's worth it because one person could make a difference.

Thank you,

Reed F.

Dear Mr. Offen,

You are the most genuine human being I've ever met or listened to . . . even though you lived through a horrific experience, you were still full of life and made many humorous comments.

With love and God Bless,

Alison S.

Dear Mr. Offen,

Thank you for making the sacrifice of reliving your horrible memories to teach me. You taught me that with Hope and Faith I can survive anything.

Sincerely,

Shawn S.

Dear Mr. Offen,

When you talked to us, I felt like I was really there and it scared me, but made me feel very humble to be in the presence of someone who went through all this. Thank you so much for sharing with us even though it must hurt very much.

Sincerely,

Lindsey V.

Dear Mr. Offen,

Even with all that I have learned about the Holocaust in school, your presentation was the best learning experience I have had on the subject.

Sincerely,

Melissa S.

Dear Mr. Offen,

You have my utmost respect and gratitude.

Sincerely,

Justin W.

Ausweis — Certification.

Herr Offen Salomon
Mister

geb. am _____ in Krakow
born _____ at Krakow

zuletzt wohnhaft _____
last domicile

wurde vom 13.3.1943. bis 5.5.1945.

in nationalsozialistischen Konzentrationslagern gefangen gehalten und vom **Konzentrationslager Mauthausen** in Freiheit gesetzt.

was kept in captivity from 13.3.1943 to 5.5.1945 in Nazi-German concentration camps and was liberated from the concentration camp of Mauthausen.

LINZ, O.Ö.

Unterschriften und Stempel:
signatures and stamps:

Lagerkomitee P
Camp Comite

Lagerkommandant
Camp commandant

Linz, am 26 JUN 1945

Provisional identifikation card for civilian internee of Mauthausen.

Vorläufige Identitätskarte für Mauthausen, Gruppe Zivilinternierte.

88593

Current number _____ Internee number
Laufende Nr. _____ Häftlings-Nr. Offen

Family name Offen
Familienname

Christian name Salomon
Vorname

Born _____ at Krakow
Geboren _____ in

Nationality Polish Jew
Nationalität

Adress Gut Harth Camp
Adresse

Fingerprint:
Fingerabdruck

Signature: Offen Salomon
Unterschrift

Linz, am 28 JUN

Sam's first I.D.
He possessed no other documentation at liberation.

These pictures were taken before the ghetto started and were used for Kennkartes. Some friends found them after the war in German archives.

(right)
Jacob Offen,
died at age 49 in
Auschwitz-Birkenau
gas chamber, Sept. 1944.

(left)
Rochme Gitel Offen,
died at age 44 in Belzec
gas chamber, Oct. 28, 1942.

(right)
Miriam Offen,
died at age 16 in Belzec
gas chamber, Oct. 28, 1942.

(left)
Yiddish letter written by Uncle Joel to family in US. (English translation on pg. 98)

(above)
Uncle Joel and family, 1937.

(above)
My mother and father on their wedding day, 1920.

(above) Mauthausen Block 5.

(bottom) Liberated prisioners at Mauthausen Death Camp. US Army photo, May 5, 1945.

(left)
Mauthausen
Death Camp.
Day of liberation,
May 5, 1945.

(right)
Donald Montgomery
American GI.
Sam's liberator.

(left)
Sam's family.

(above) Sam in London.

(above) Passover Seder meal in
Allied Jewish Soldier's Club.
Bari, Italy, 1945.

(right)
Hyla's family.

(above) Sam and Donald Montgomery reunited in Michigan, October, 1993.

(below) "KL" stands for "concentration camp" in German. Branding occured in the salt mine in Wieliczka, near Krakow, Poland.

(left)
The three brothers
return to Auschwitz in
2001 to memorial sites.

(right)
Offen Family
Roots Tour.
Return to Poland
to childhood
home, 1985.

(left)
Hyla and
Sam's Golden
Wedding
Anniversary,
June 19, 2002.

(left)
Kaddish (prayer for the dead). Praying with a picture of my mother. Belzec, 1985.

(right)
Majdanek Camp, 1985.

(left)
Sam behind gate to former Belzec Death Camp where his mother and sister perished. Belzec, 2001.

(*left*)
Sam and high school group after a presentation at the Holocaust Memorial Center, 2005.

(*right*)
Sam at Whitwell, Tennessee with students by cattle car filled with 18 million paper clips, 2005.

(left) One of Sam's favorite avocations.

(above) Sam at 2005 Krakow-Schindler's List Reunion, Miami, Florida with Doug Greenberg, Director of the Shoah Foundation.

(above) Gloria and Nathan, Krysia and Bernard, Sam and Hyla, 2005.

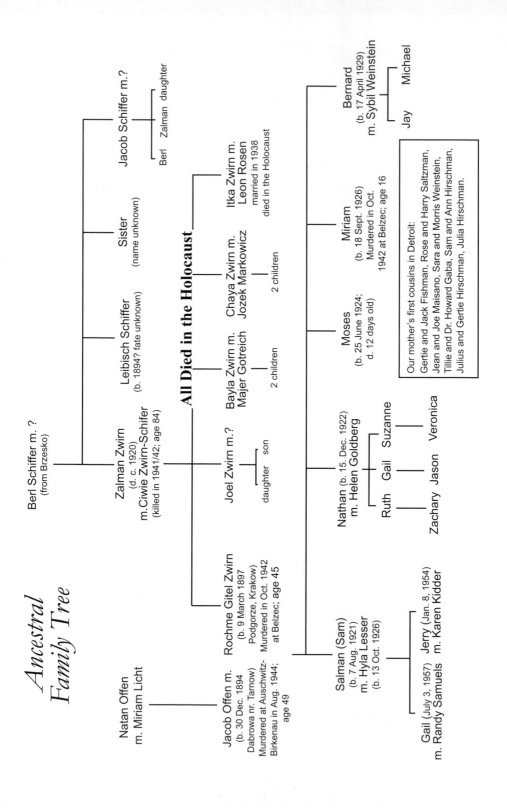

Ancestral Family Tree

Natan Offen
m. Miriam Licht

Berl Schiffer m. ?
(from Brzesko)

Jacob Offen m.
(b. 30 Dec. 1894
Dabrowa nr. Tarnow)
Murdered at Auschwitz-
Birkenau in Aug. 1944;
age 49

Rochme Gitel Zwirn
(b. 9 March 1897
Podgorze, Krakow)
Murdered in Oct. 1942
at Belzec; age 45

Zalman Zwirn
(d. c. 1920)
m. Ciwie Zwirn-Schifer
(killed in 1941/42; age 84)

Leibisch Schiffer
(b. 1894? fate unknown)

Sister
(name unknown)

Jacob Schiffer m. ?

Berl   Zalman   daughter

All Died in the Holocaust

Bayla Zwirn m.
Majer Gotreich

2 children

Chaya Zwirn m.
Jozek Markowicz

2 children

Itka Zwirn m.
Leon Rosen
married in 1938
died in the Holocaust

Joel Zwirn m. ?

daughter   son

Salman (Sam)
(b. 7 Aug. 1921)
m. Hyla Lesser
(b. 13 Oct. 1926)

Nathan (b. 15. Dec. 1922)
m. Helen Goldberg

Moses
(b. 25 June 1924;
d. 12 days old)

Miriam
(b. 18 Sept. 1926)
Murdered in Oct.
1942 at Belzec; age 16

Bernard
(b. 17 April 1929)
m. Sybil Weinstein

Jay   Michael

Gail (July 3, 1957)
m. Randy Samuels

Jerry (Jan. 8, 1954)
m. Karen Kidder

Ruth   Gail   Suzanne

Zachary   Jason   Veronica

Our mother's first cousins in Detroit:
Gertie and Jack Fishman, Rose and Harry Saltzman,
Jean and Joe Maisano, Sara and Morris Weinstein,
Tillie and Dr. Howard Gaba, Sam and Ann Hirschman,
Julius and Gertie Hirschman, Julia Hirschman.